Prayer on Wings

A search for authentic prayer

by Carolyn Stahl Bohler

San Diego, California

LuraMedia ™

Cover Design by Carol Jeanotilla, Denver, Colorado

LuraMedia
7060 Miramar Road, Suite 104
San Diego, CA 92121

Library of Congress Cataloging-in-Publication Data

Bohler, Carolyn Stahl.
    Prayer on wings: a search for authentic prayer /
Carolyn Stahl Bohler.
       p. cm.
    Includes bibliographical references.
    Includes index.
    ISBN 0-931055-72-5
    1. Prayer — Christianity. I. Title
BV215.S74   1990
248.3'2 — dc20   89-28468
                                           CIP

CREDITS

Grateful acknowledgment is made to the following copyright holders for permission to use their copyrighted material:

Cynthia D. Alte, for the quotations from materials written for the course, "Christian Prayer: Expanded Options," taught by Kathryn Robotham at United Theological Seminary, Dayton, Ohio, Spring, 1986.

Beacon Press, for the following quotations:
    From BEYOND GOD THE FATHER by Mary Daly. Copyright 1973 by Beacon Press.
    From TOWARD A NEW PSYCHOLOGY OF WOMEN by Jean Baker Miller, Second Edition. Copyright 1986 by Beacon Press.
    From THE JOURNEY IS HOME by Nelle Morton. Copyright 1985, by Beacon Press.
    From SEXISM AND GOD-TALK by Rosemary Radford Ruether. Copyright 1983, by Beacon Press.

Harper & Row, Publishers, Inc., for the following quotations:
    From SOPHIA: THE FUTURE OF FEMINIST SPIRITUALITY by Susan Cady, Marian Ronan, and Hal Taussig. Copyright ©1986 by the authors. (Retitled WISDOM'S FEAST: SOPHIA IN STUDY AND CELEBRATION, 1989.) Reprinted by permisssion of Harper & Row, Publishers, Inc.
    From WOMEN AND RELIGION: A FEMINIST SOURCEBOOK OF CHRISTIAN THOUGHT by Elizabeth Clark and Herbert Richardson.

ACKNOWLEDGMENTS

The ideas in this book began to form when I served on the staff of the School of Theology at Claremont, California, working on what was called the "Burning Bush Project." Members from more than ten churches explored, with the seminary students and faculty, the interconnection of spirituality and global responsibility. As I led workshops and listened, I heard questions and issues people raised as they prayed. For my dissertation in the Ph.D. program at the School of Theology at Claremont I wrote *The Politics of Prayer.* Howard Clinebell, John Cobb, Patricia Hodges, and Donald Rhoades were outstanding coaches — urging me to find my own niche as I spoke out of both the psychological and theological disciplines. Penny Matthews, Linda Terril, and Nelle Morton were influential in my thinking and practice.

The church members and ecumenical community where I served the Mission Hills United Methodist Church in San Diego, California, eagerly cooperated with my explorations of prayer. Members participated in what we called "Prayer Empowerment Groups" to practice using styles of prayer and metaphors for the Deity. Aileen Kerby, Paula Doss, and Phyllis Vodicka are spiritually questioning women who worked with me closely.

Clergywomen in the California Pacific Annual Conference of the United Methodist Church were quite supportive. They provided anecdotes and personal stories, as well as challenging ideas. Patricia Farris, Phyllis Tyler-Wayman, Karen Scheib, and Gwen Jones-Lurvey were especially helpful.

Preston Price, a neighbor clergyperson in San Diego, read a draft of this work and began implementing many ideas with the members of a prayer group in his church. He shared with me their responses, helping to convince me of the importance of this work.

When I moved to Ohio there were many in the Midwest who were interested and supportive. Several groups of pastors asked me to offer lectures or retreats, during which the ideas for this book continued to take shape. I especially recall an East Ohio 1986 United Methodist clergy event which became a think tank on the topic of metaphors for the Deity: People were alive with possibilities. Students, faculty, and alums at the United Church of Christ United Theological Seminary of the Twin Cities, Minneapolis (1983); Northern Illinois United Methodist clergy (1984); Central Pennsylvania United Methodist clergy (1985); Iowa United Methodist clergy (1985); Roman Catholic students and faculty of St. Meinrad Seminary (1987); and Kansas United Methodist clergy (1988) heard my ideas at various stages and responded generously.

My colleagues in the American Association of Pastoral Counselors (1986) received with keen interest my ideas on the psychological implications of prayer for women and men and offered me many ideas. More recently Carroll Saussy, a professor at Wesley Theological Seminary in Washington, D.C., read chapters of this work and gave me critical reflections.

Members of the United Theological Seminary community in Dayton,

Ohio, have been involved in this work. Motivation to write was one of the many gifts provided by women in formal and informal support groups that included Cyndi Raske, Phyllis Schaefer, Marilyn Evans, Rae Lynn Schaef, Julie Hostetter, Harriet Miller, and Linda Marshall.

When I taught classes entitled "Christian Prayer: Expanded Options," and "Theory and Practice of Pastoral and Personal Prayer," the students' exploration inspired me greatly and taught me much. Particular students of the United Theological Seminary community were of special help: Lynda Hamilton, Patricia Glover, Annette Dimond, David Gehret, Lois Buchholz, EunHae Kee, and Patricia Bloom. Byron George and Tracy Taylor did research for me at critical moments.

Kathy Farmer and Kendal McCabe were patient with me when I telephoned them with questions of their disciplines. I thank Ed Wheeler for giving time to reading the manuscript and Patricia Linnemann for many hallway talks on the subject. Robert Simmons and I co-led a workshop for West Ohio Urban Ministers; in the preparation for that Robert helped me to see that the issues of prayer I raise here are important for African-Americans and indeed were an integral part of African-American History. Marti Anderson provided indispensable secretarial help.

Ellen Kubay Adkins reminded me that "I have all the time I need."

I thank my family: my sister for reading a draft; my children, for their interest, patience, and permission to use them as examples; and my husband, for reading about ten drafts and for learning through the years the wonderful art of how to offer editorial comments in ways I could hear them.

Finally, I thank Lura Geiger, publisher, and Patricia Backman, editor, for sharing the sense of importance of this topic and enabling this book to be born.

So many friends and fellow-seekers gave generously of their time, beliefs, support, and care. I thank them all.

Carolyn Stahl Bohler
Dayton, Ohio
October 1989

Dedicated to
Lysbeth and Ben Stahl
who encouraged us to find our own ways

CONTENTS

*"O Jerusalem, Jerusalem, killing the prophets
and stoning those who are sent to you! How often
would I have gathered your children together as a
hen gathers her brood under her wings . . ."*

(Luke 13:34)

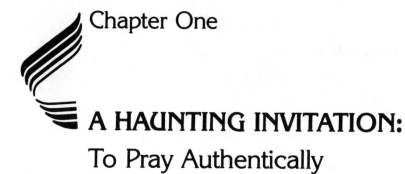

Chapter One

A HAUNTING INVITATION:
To Pray Authentically

Wanting to Pray

Infinite and Intimate Friend:

I sit with You in silence . . .
Imagining Your Presence
 like a Light shining brightly through every
  being,
 like a Whirlwind disturbing the status quo,
 like a Mother and Father holding us until
  there is peace.
May I learn how to pray —
 to receive Your Guidance,
 to be shaped by that Wisdom,
 and to act upon it.
I let Your Light shine through me, and I see it
 in others.
I trust Your Wind to blow to transform the
 world, including myself.
I accept Your Love which unfolds peace.
Amen.

A woman was silent as around her hundreds of people prayed the Lord's Prayer in their native languages: Tongan, Spanish, Korean, Japanese, Native American, English, and others. The worship leader had suggested that each person pray in her or his own language. This silent woman was deterred by the opening words, "Our Father." For her, that prayer language had become inauthentic. In telling me about this event, she explained, "to pray in my own language has become a haunting invitation. I hardly know how to proceed, and silence seems the best approach I might make in the moment."

A disciple who wanted to know more about prayer asked Jesus, "Lord, teach us to pray, as John taught his disciples" (Luke 11:1). Jesus' answer was, translated from Aramaic, "When ye pray, say, 'Our Father which art in heaven, hallowed be thy name . . .'" That "Lord's Prayer" has been recited during many a childbirth, at countless bedsides, in myriad dangers and amidst joyous celebrations. Yet one prayer cannot meet everyone's prayer needs all the time. We need to ask again and again, "Teach us to pray." And our answers must come out of the wrestlings which take place within each of us. As we work to discover how to pray, we work together, and we commune with the Spirit of God which is in our midst today.

Authentic prayer is prayer in your own words, out of sincere longings and based upon views of God which you genuinely believe. This book is for those who, like the silenced woman, are ready to follow an invitation to discover for themselves how to pray authentically. In prayer, as in any act, you have the right and responsibility to ask questions, to reflect, to be sure that what you are doing fits what you truly believe about the Deity, about yourself, and about each other. At first the thought of questioning our prayer practices and beliefs may seem like an enormous task. But the following pages will address issues one at a time, gradually noting how they interrelate. This chapter asks what occurs when you pray. In the next three chapters attention will be given to God — how you conceptualize and name the One with Whom you pray. The various ways you name God affects you as an individual and us as a community. The third main focus of this book is the style of prayer — do you use words, pray in silence or action, or enlist your imagination when you pray?

This search for authentic prayer is crucial, because of all the dimensions of religious life, prayer is the one which is least inspected. We discuss in great detail how to structure and organize churches; we debate and take stands on social issues. We read and reread the Bible, grasping new understandings, but we tend to repeat the routines of prayer (or avoid them) as if they were fixed in concrete. Prayer ought to expand as people grow. We can build upon the past, but we need to be open to the future. Prayer is a living and dynamic activity. It can be — should be — an adventure.

Although written prayers from our tradition are useful, the biggest lesson for us to learn about prayer is to be free to pray in our rooms — when we have shut the doors (Matthew 6:6). Prayer which has been meaningful for millions may still be of great value today, although its value differs from person to person. But we need not pray in a certain way solely because that is the way it has been done. We need to pray from our own situations and current needs, thoughts, and feelings.

Many think prayer is necessarily a holy, righteous act; this is not so. Prayer is an act much like any other act; we can enter into it (and exit from it) stuck in old ways and centered in our own wants. For example, I could pray for health, but consciously ignore body signals which are ways God is communicating action I must take to be healthy. I could pray to be more loving, but refuse to read or listen to perspectives different from my own which may change some of my prejudices. I could pray in public with greater concern for the effect upon the listeners than upon my sincerity with God. I could pray for the good of one person at the expense of another, without being sensitive to the needs of all concerned. Such prayer is unholy and self-righteous rather than righteous.

Prayer *is* holy, if it is done with a desire to be open to Divine Guidance and a desire to act wisely. My prayer for health could lead me toward a deeper appreciation of my body and greater sensitivity to my body's messages. My prayer to be more loving may be one factor which helps me to grasp the perspectives of others who are different from myself. My public prayer may speak sincerely from my struggles and, because of that, affect others. And my prayer for another may create in me a larger picture of the situation and greater caring for everyone involved.

All too often people continue to pray in empty or alienating ways — or give up on prayer — simply because they do not know that there are other options or do not experience inner permission to explore those options. It is important to see how prayer affects women and men and what can be done to increase the effectiveness of prayer for all of us. People are quite different; what meets one person's spiritual needs will not necessarily meet those of another. However, all of us would benefit from expanding our practice of prayer in two directions: to use many more metaphors for the Deity (working to grasp the implications of the metaphors which we use) and to explore a variety of ways we might pray, that is, prayer styles.

The Lord's Prayer uses the metaphor "Father" for the Deity. If it were prayed amidst a liturgy in church in which the congregation also prayed, "Womb of God, help us to feel Your nurturance surrounding us," the Lord's Prayer would be seen as one model, with one metaphor for the Deity; it would not be seen as the only way to pray. The Lord's Prayer uses language which was not authentic for the woman at the multicultural worship service. Silence may be what she needs now. But it could happen that she would move out of silence to explore many other prayer options; then, at times the Lord's Prayer might be useful again.

Think of the task as "expanding" our prayer, rather than "changing" our way of praying. Change implies that what is being practiced is wrong. It is wrong only in that it is limited. The challenge is to expand our horizons, to open ourselves to greater possibilities.

It is more important to reflect upon the variety of prayers prayed individually and in corporate worship than it is to investigate any one particular prayer. This book looks at prayer in its diversity; it does not look at any one prayer to determine whether it is authentic or appropriate by itself.

DEFINITION OF PRAYER

My working definition of prayer is "conscious communication with the Deity." While I am convinced that we are communicating with the Deity at all times, even when we are not conscious of it, I am only labeling as prayer those times in which we have decided to become aware of that communication. People who pray vary in their perception of the direction and mode of communication in prayer. Some emphasize humans talking with God; some stress God's communication to humans; others perceive a two-way sharing. Some assume prayer must use words, while others stress silence or imaginative activities. But virtually all people who pray conceive of prayer within a framework of communication.[1]

"With the Deity" is included in the definition of prayer because I do believe that there is some reality which is within us and beyond us, with which we do communicate. I frequently use the term "Deity" rather than the more well-used term "God" because "God" has a definite, while often unconscious, masculine association. "Deity" expands the concept, enabling Christians to think more broadly than they generally do. I virtually never use the word "Deity" to begin a prayer. I use it to think abstractly about the Deity, but seldom as a name or metaphor when I speak to God.

INTERDEPENDENCE WITH THE DEITY

I believe that the relationship between the Deity and humans is one of interdependence. When you pray, more than at any other time, this interdependence becomes essential to consider because there is the expectation that as the Deity or the human communicates, the other responds in some fashion. Yet, many people express in their prayers what sounds more like a dependent relationship than an interdependent one.

Some people believe that their piety increases the more that they can claim to be absolutely dependent upon God. But effective prayer involves the sharing of mutual responsibilities with our Co-Worker. When you pray for a loved one's health, you ought to assume that you will continue to care and to act wisely even as you expect God to do God's part. For example, along with the prayer, you continue to bring liquids, to help with the other's work, or to offer transportation. This co-worker mentality is obvious, too, when you pray for yourself. You work with God as you seek what to do in your relationships, regarding your body, or in your social responsibilities. Calling God "Father" and "Lord" can inhibit our realization of interdependence. There is little expectation in our prayers and little representation in our images used for the Deity (until the concept of father becomes less stereotyped) that the Deity also depends upon us. If we are ill, exhausted, confused, or hardly able to discern for what to pray, we may conceive of the Spiritual Presence in a way which shows primarily dependence. As a temporary stage we may be strengthened and nurtured by relying upon God thought of as a parent upon whom to depend. But when strength is revived and guidance received, we need to move once again toward a more interdependent way of praying with the Deity.

God is not wholly dependent upon you, just as you are not merely a dependent. God wills and acts on God's own. Yet as God interrelates to the world, God's will is only fully effected when the world responds. So-called miracles may be times when people — beside themselves with pain and doubt or filled with faith — open to a huge influx of God's power. Even if you do not respond openly to God, God still tries to persuade you and the world to prepare for God's desires to be fulfilled on earth.

When you acknowledge your interdependence with God, you can sense power in your prayer. When you pray the following prayer, you do not abdicate power but enhance it by joining with God's power. You do not diminish your own responsibility by handing the situation over to God but rather increase your awareness of your need to cooperate with God to accomplish the good.

Our Co-Authored Script

Co-Author of Life Divine:

May I cooperate with Your ideas for me. May the story You are able to write through me be one filled with spirit, one filled with compassion, one worthy of others' readings.

May my life be one which gives a touch of gentleness to the world. But let me know the difference between gentleness and the avoidance of conflict. May I risk doing what is unpopular, if that needs to be expressed through me.

May I trust Your Co-Authorship and be able to see when I deviate too far from the story You would like my presence to tell.

May I see Your part in the story of others, Your ideas in the mysteries, comedies and tragedies which I observe. I know that we all do not "live happily ever after," but may we live courageously and more closely to Your creative and always relevant ideas for our script. Amen.

Although many of us tend to pray with too much emphasis upon what we want God to do in prayer, that is, we act very dependent, at other times we feel as if we are independent of God, on our own. When we feel the burden of making things happen as if we were the creator, we can remind ourselves of the inter-dependence with the Deity and consciously think of letting God become more involved in our lives. Once when I wrestled to sense what was my responsibility and what was God's, I playfully but sincerely prayed this prayer.

I'm Grown Up, but Still 2½

Mother-Father God:

> *Let me do it myself!*
> *I want to do it.*
> *Help me.*
> *No, I want to.*
> *Show me.*

WHEN WE PRAY

According to our needs, moods, and surroundings, we pray in a variety of styles. I might repeat, "calm, calm, calm," in the midst of a heated debate, or if I have been very busy, I might find a spot where I can sit to practice silence. When in need of sensing a close Divine relationship, I talk with God. In an emergency which involves someone's health, I tend to visualize wholeness. I might join hands and walk with a woman who tells me she was abused and needs to act to take control of her life. As we walk and talk I may think of God many times — the prayer is a thought of God combined with action.

Think of yourself in prayer as opening yourself up consciously to Divine Guidance. There is a concentration upon the interaction of the Deity, yourself, and the others about whom you are praying. Consequently, barriers between God and yourself, such as a sense of isolation or an attachment to the past, are broken down. Prayer can be sheer openness, with no agenda on your part. This side of prayer might be called "receptive" prayer. This prayer may "end" without any concrete guidance knowingly received, but there has been a time of concentrated attention to the relationship between yourself and the Deity and often a rededication to be attentive to God's guidance.

There is also what I call "directive" prayer in which you think of a concrete situation which pertains to another or yourself. When you are directive in prayer, you need not "tell" God what to do or what you want to happen; rather, you can firmly recognize that God wants the very best to occur for all who are involved in the situation. As you acknowledge that God wants the best, and that in the current situation, God knows what would be the best, you can spiritually put yourself in accord with whatever that best is, to be known as it unfolds. You are in effect "voting" for God's way and yielding or relinquishing barriers to that result.

For example, it may happen that a father begins a prayer for his teenaged daughter by asking that she stop seeing a particular friend. But, during or after the prayer, he receives promptings which lead him to trust his daughter and to get to know the friend. If he tells God what to do, his prayer would be something like, "God, let my daughter see that this relationship is not good for her." A prayer which "votes" for God's way would be, "God, I am open to Your guidance, as I guide my daughter. Please let her choose her friends wisely and enable me to know what to do to help in that process. If she needs to let go of the friendship which she now has, may she have the wisdom and courage to do that, and if I can help in that process, I know that You are teaching me how, and I am ready to learn."

We can err. We do not have to accept God's guidance fully. God longs and empowers all involved to see and to act, but all are free. Prayer can work as a kind of alignment in which we shift ourselves over to God's perspective, seeking to follow the best God offers.

Therefore, prayer alters our relationship to God by making us more open to God's guidance. But it also affects others, partly because we will act, think, and feel differently about them and their situations (we are more likely to think of them combined with the idea of God guiding their lives), but also because we are adding "mental" or "spiritual" force to God's guidance. We are letting our concern be transformed into trust, expecting that God is involved and committing ourselves to do all we can to respond effectively.

The outcome of prayer is never fully known. All prayer is "answered" in that we are engaged with the Divine Source, offering longings and receiving understandings. But the exact answers to precise questions are mixed up with many other events. For example, a woman who prays for wisdom in relating to her family members may include a specific request that her son stay in college. She may find that the specific prayer regarding college is not "answered" in that he leaves college. But the mother nevertheless feels a deeper trust that God is working in the family. She is calm, trusting that her son will find his way in life and that she will be able to relate well to him.

The prayer is answered, and that answer is not just, "No." The "answer" to her prayer is her own trust in God to direct the situation, her trust in her son to be receptive to God's guidance, and her peace of mind in relating to her son. But the prayer need not have affected just her; it affects her son and all others involved as well. They have been cared for and provided with an extra dose of love and encouragement to follow the wisdom which God is seeking to give.

Answers sometimes occur while praying — as when an image of a dove occurred to a woman when she visualized a relationship, enabling her to sense deep within that there was potential for peace in that relationship. But often answers occur in the ensuing days, when we are not consciously communicating with the Deity, but we are attentive to the avenues through which God communicates. This is quite similar to a counseling session, which seldom by itself gives the answers to the problems or growth-needs of the counselee. Rather, the life of the counselee will evoke answers subsequent to the session. The counseling session offers a slight reorientation of experience and perspective. So, too, prayer seldom yields answers instantly, but rather in a manner which unfolds in the future.

Prayer changes things. At the very least it changes the perspective of the one who prays, and that is an enormous gift. There are so many people with a variety of thoughts and feelings about any given situation; some of these thoughts and feelings knowingly or unknowingly thwart or further God's will. Prayer could tilt the weight of all these thoughts and feelings toward responding positively to God's guidance. Prayer encourages love and empathy for others as it moves us from our solo perspectives to a much larger view.

EXPRESSING EMOTIONS IN PRAYER

In the prayer on page 9 entitled "I'm Grown Up, but Still 2½," I was in a rambunctious mood, with a mixture of serious pondering and rebelliousness. I believe that it is all right to pray in such a mood; in fact, it is appropriate to pray in *any* mood and to express *any* emotion we are experiencing. Some prayers in this book were prayed while I was sad, angry, frustrated, in mourning, upset. Others were prayed when I was awestruck, grateful, thankful, and filled with love.

Emotions are gifts from God as surely as thoughts are. The ability to feel is as sacred as the capacity to think. It is regrettable when people feel that they are too angry, too jealous, or even too much in love to pray. I believe God feels and God can feel our feelings. We do not need to "protect" God from any aspect of ourselves, nor can we hide any emotion from God!

The disciples prayed while they were experiencing both the deep bond of friendship and anticipated grief at what we call the "Last Supper." Jesus prayed on a mountain in such an ecstatic state that his countenance is said to have altered (Luke 9:29). Yet, in a very different emotional state, he prayed with some doubt about God's will in the Garden of Gethsemane, "My Father, if it be possible, let this cup pass from me; nevertheless, not as I will, but as thou wilt." (Matthew 26:39). Out of pain and anguish on the cross, he prayed, "My God, my God, why hast thou forsaken me?" (Matthew 27:46).

Authenticity in prayer includes not trying to hide. To be authentic before God includes not only praying in whatever prayer style seems appropriate, using whatever metaphor for the Deity which enables us to experience that Deity, but also expressing honestly our emotions in the moments of the prayer. Our emotions themselves may undergo a transformation while we pray, just as our attitudes or understandings are altered during the course of, and due to, the prayer.

The way emotions affect our prayer differs according to the format or style of prayer we use. The act of sitting in silence or repeating a phrase is calming for the vast majority of people. Therefore, whether we begin in anger, ecstatically in love, resentful, or curious, our silence or our repetition of words tends to soothe us, to bring us to a milder, more peaceful state. For this reason, these styles of prayer are good to use when that calm state is sought.

However, prayer need not lead away from intensity of emotion. It can evoke strong emotions. Imagery prayer, like nighttime dreams, has the potential for arousing a variety of emotions which can lead to wisdom regarding what we should do or how we feel.

An instructive imagery prayer of mine years ago worried me, for it led me to realize that I *felt* barren. I visualized Jesus the Christ handing me seeds to plant. In my imagination I did plant them in a tilled garden, but nothing would grow in that mental scene. I could not will the image to change. That prayer did not make me feel good — it saddened me. But, it also eventually inspired me to take some action in my life to plant seeds which could be more fertile.

People have shared with me their embarrassment over visualizing Jesus the Christ in romantic ways in their imagery prayer. There are different kinds of love, but there are no walls between them, so that when we allow symbolic images to arise, it is quite understandable that love can show up in different forms.

Some people report feeling guilty even attempting to pray when they are in emotional states which they deem unworthy of prayer. If you are in such a state, I suggest that you start the prayer by stating your discomfort with your emotions as you pray, but state also your longing to pray anyway. In this way, you are acknowledging (to God, but also to yourself) what you are embarrassed or worried about. That acknowledgment is often enough to help you let go of the concern, to let the rest of the prayer continue spontaneously.

THE PRAYERS IN THIS BOOK

The prayers which are interspersed throughout this book seek to exemplify the ideas which I am communicating throughout the text. Some prayers are quite specific, such as several relating to children and to health. But many prayers are more general, applicable for many people under a wide spectrum of circumstances. Some of the prayers have been my own, for myself. Some are prayers I have prayed in "intercession" for others. Still others were written as though I were another, praying from that perspective. Therefore, although I am the author of all of the prayers, the experiences which they reveal are varied.

I would be disappointed if these prayers were taken as static models of how an individual ought to pray. It is precisely the point of this book that we need to find our own ways to pray and that we need not take what is given us as the norm. We must explore, search, and give birth to our own genuine prayers. I offer these as prayer teasers, as fluid or dynamic models, to help break loose from past forms of prayer, stereotyped words for prayer, or a limited set of metaphors for the Deity.

The goal is to move away from external authority to your own internal Deity-rooted authority. A paradox of this book is that it offers examples of *my* own way of praying to encourage you to explore *your* own way of praying. The best prayer is one that is genuinely yours.

FOR REFLECTION AND ACTION

1. Recall a few vivid memories of times during your life when you prayed. What makes those moments stand out for you? (e.g., you felt very alone; you received a dramatic answer; you realized you felt distant from or close to God; you were ecstatic; you felt powerless.)

2. Recall messages which you received as a child and while you were growing up about how you were supposed to pray. Ask yourself critically now which of those words of advice enable you to pray authentically today and which hinder your praying. (e.g., My Sunday school teacher told me to close my eyes when I prayed, but I often pray now with my eyes open, enjoying and experiencing the environment in which I pray.)

3. How would you, with your current experience, teach a child to pray? How would you explain the interaction between God and people in prayer?

4. Notice how you name God when you think about praying. Let yourself experience where you are on the dependent-inter-dependent-independent spectrum in relation to God. Do you feel yourself to be completely dependent upon God, so inde-pendent of God that you don't pray, or interdependent?

5. Notice some dominant emotions present in your prayers. Ponder whether there are any emotional states in which you do not feel inclined to pray. Why?

NOTES

1. For Karl Barth, renowned neoorthodox theologian in the mid-decades of this century, explicit prayer must be a bold and genuine asking. We are free to pray, to ask for anything, as long as we use words and ask. He was opposed to the use of imagery, silence, and repeated phrases as prayer because he did not see these as asking of God. It is clear that for Barth, communication in prayer is from humans to the Deity and discursive in style. (Karl Barth, *Church Dogmatics* [Edinburgh: Clark, 1961] III/4, 89-115 and Karl Barth, *Prayer* [Philadelphia: Westminster Press, 1946] 27-28.)

    A much different view of prayer was presented by the early nineteenth century theologian, Friedrich Schleiermacher. He understood Christian prayer to be "joining the thought of God with every thought of any importance that occurs to us." We are to maintain a "God-consciousness." We are not to ask. We are either to give thanks or to resign ourselves to the situation. Schleiermacher's theology is based firmly on a view of foreordination which indicates that everything that happens is indeed God's will. Therefore it would be foolish to ask for anything, since it might be something which is not according to God's will, and if that is the case, it would not happen anyway. He allows for "wish-making" prayers, but does so only because he knows people cannot refrain from praying in this manner. He would prefer that we grow beyond this need to wish or ask. For Schleiermacher, then, prayer is primarily communication from God to humans. We are to receive gratefully or wrestle in order to become grateful. Anything which we would communicate to God would be superfluous. (Friedrich Schleiermacher, *Selected Sermons* [New York: Funk and Wagnalls, ©1928, 1976] 39 and Friedrich Schleiermacher, *The Christian Faith* [Philadelphia: Fortress, 1928] 456, 669-674.)

    Because theologian Paul Tillich did not think of the Deity as a noun, a "Being," but rather "Being Itself," he could say, "If it (prayer) is brought down to the level of a conversation between two beings, it is blasphemous and ridiculous." The purpose of prayer is "to reunite the creature with its creative ground." Therefore, prayer need not take on any one style or form, but ought to be "authentic." An inauthentic prayer would copy the surfaces without expressing depth, such as when someone else's words are used and repeated by the one who prays without any encounter with the Ground of Being directly. If prayer is authentic there is an ecstatic encounter, a movement out of oneself to transcend the subject-object nature of the God-human relationship. One is reunited with the Spiritual Presence. God functions as a directing creativity which works through us as we are receptive to it and willing to be shaped by it. So, for Tillich, prayer is a two-directional encounter, but it ought to go beyond dialogue, to the experience of the Deity as involved in one's own ongoing creativity. (Paul Tillich, *Systematic Theology* [Chicago: University of Chicago Press, 1967] I, 127 and III, 64.)

    John Cobb, a process theologian, considers prayer to be the "whole stance of openness to God and responsiveness to the divine call." Many styles of prayer are advocated by process theologians, for each style would foster a different way of receiving God's guidance. Prayer is really correct alignment. We are "to align ourselves with the directions in which God is already drawing us." (Harry James Cargus and Bernard Lee (eds.), *Religious Experience and Process Theology* [New York: Paulist Press, 1976] 363 and John B. Cobb, Jr., *To Pray or Not to Pray* [Nashville: The Upper Room, 1974] 18.)

Chapter Two

TWIN SPIRITUAL NEEDS:

To Be "Like" and "With" the Infinite Friend

Wanting a Bigger God

Black God:

When I name You, I think that You are out there
— radically other than me.
> But I sense that You are hidden deep
> within me, too.
You have supported friends through long hard
years, providing hope and joy in the midst of
much struggle.
> For me You are mystery, beauty, just
> becoming known.
> May I learn to know You, Black God, Black
> Goddess.
> May I grow big enough in the size of spirit
> to feel Your warmth, to sense
> Your guidance.
> May I hear You and see You in others, our
> world, and in myself. Amen.

An African-American university administrator noted with pride that his two-year-old son identified with black children in magazines and on television. His son seemed to be developing a good sense of self-esteem. The administrator also noted that the son's best friend was a three-year-old white boy. The father hoped that as his son grew, he would continue to identify positively with African-Americans and to have friendships with people of different colors.

We identify and we affiliate; we are "like" others and "with" others. The degree to which we meet these needs for "likeness" and "withness" affects our self-image and our interpersonal relationships. But we do not just need to be like and with other people, we also have deep twin spiritual needs to be "like" and "with" the Deity. These needs are seldom lifted up as ones which we fulfill intentionally, but they are powerful needs, and we work hard at an unconscious level to meet them, or suffer from their remaining unmet.

IDENTIFICATION

We all experience identification with other people. We see people we admire, form an emotional tie with them, and try to be like them. The process continues all our lives and it starts early. When my four-year-old daughter saw a ballet on television, she rushed to put on her tights and danced around the living room while she watched the professionals perform. When her younger brother saw the applause she got, he joined in the dance, mimicking his sister.

Identification can empower us: We see another who is like us in some ways doing something quite well, receiving the plaudits of others, and we feel encouraged to reach for goals that we might have thought out of reach. African-Americans gained confidence, greater self-esteem, and a greater sense of internal power when Jesse Jackson sought the nomination for the Presidency of the United States. Similarly, Geraldine Ferraro running for the Vice Presidency of the United States and Corazon Aquino assuming leadership of the Philippines provided women in both countries with a greater sense of their own value, responsibility, and power.

Clearly, identification is strongest when there is gender likeness or ethnic and cultural similarity. I experienced the strength of gender identification vividly when I heard a woman seminary professor speak at a gathering of clergywomen, when clergywomen and women professors were still quite few in number. I had heard hundreds of lectures by men, but when I heard her speak, I experienced a new sense of empowerment. I had previously identified to a degree across gender with male professors, but identification with her clarified my goals and made them appear more attainable.

Yet the process of developing identifications is not entirely left up to the individual. Our culture bombards us with images with which we are urged or expected to identify. Some of the messages are so insistent and so frequent that a degree of identification occurs without our realizing it. We think we have ignored or rejected images constructed by a particular commercial, only to find ourselves gravitating toward that product when we go to the store.

Similarly, when we are growing up we may take pride in how different we are from our mother or father, how much of an independent existence we are creating for ourselves. Yet we discover that some of those attributes we rejected in our parents have become part of our own personality when we are older.

At times the way a person identifies with others could be unhealthy. For example, I could over-identify with another. I may want so much to be like my sister that I have difficulty deciding who is she and who am I. Also, it is possible to lose balance with our identifications. Sometimes, it is healthy to identify with the alienated, in order to stay aware of our own need to belong. But it would not be healthy to identify with those who are alienated all of the time. A person who so identifies needs to discover and cherish the "accepted" — the belonging side — in herself or himself. Likewise, we can benefit from some identifications with those who are admired, but if we only identified with heroes and heroines, we might be driven in a pathetic way toward perfection or success.

While many of us are preoccupied with identification during our teenage and young adult years, the process of identification continues throughout our lifetimes. Some people are affected by important identifications when they are forty or fifty. We continually encounter new images and new role models. We discard or modify old, irrelevant identifications and accept new ones. Identification is a lifelong dynamic process.

Our relationship with the Deity is also dynamic. We might not think that we would ever identify with the Deity. It is too powerful, too beyond our reach. But because the Deity is so awesome to conceptualize, we do so by thinking of God as possessing some attributes which we can recognize. Thus the Deity is thought of as loving, for example. Our love between parent and child, between two lovers, between friends, is different in some ways from how we think the Deity loves, but it is also like it in other ways. The more we think of God's loving, the more we realize that we can be loving, too. We recognize that although there are many ways we are NOT like the Deity, we are like God in some significant ways.

Obviously, identification with the Deity in no way means that we try to become God or pretend that we are God. Rare people who over-identify with the Deity — thinking themselves to *be* the Deity or having a difficult time distinguishing themselves from the Deity — need psychological assistance. Therapeutic work needs to be done to help the person dis-identify, to recognize his or her distinction from the Deity.

That we were made in the image and likeness of God is a major premise of our Judeo-Christian tradition. We possess some god-like qualities which we are expected to develop. We develop those very qualities in part by reminding ourselves of our likeness.

Sunday school teachers may begin us on our journey toward identification with an image of the Deity if they write the term "God" on the board and ask for qualities which the students think God has. Children yell out: "Loving, Forgiving, Wise, Father, Powerful, Jesus, Patient." The teacher is likely to proceed further in the lesson, suggesting that the children live out many of these god-like qualities. The children are encouraged to be like God both emotionally and behaviorally: for example, to feel loving and forgiving, to act forgivingly and wisely. Identification is being taught, in line with the teaching of Ephesians 5:1: "Therefore be imitators of God, as beloved children." Of course there is no thought that the children should imitate God in all ways. They are not encouraged to think they could be everywhere present or that they could exert enormous persuasive power.

The four prayers which follow begin with very different images of the Deity and have moods which are affected by those images. The situations in which the individuals pray vary, and the way they conceive of God enables them to believe that they can be empowered by God in those situations. Note for yourself images of God with which you can best identify.

Being a Father

Father in Heaven:

I need all the guidance I can have as I father my children. May I discern Your wisdom as I find my special way of caring and challenging our children. May I let go of other people's notions of what a father is enough to find out for myself what I need to be to them. May I be gentle and warm, in right doses. May I know how to limit and how to teach. May I coordinate my work with my father-hood, so that I can create in both arenas. May I have time to play, to be alone, and to have other friends, too. May I be like my father, if that is right for my children and myself, but may I know how to be different, if that is needed. I thank You, for Your infinite wisdom. Amen.

Leaving

Mother God:

I feel crushed to leave my son while he cries for me to stay, yet I must at times. He's in his father's care, a precious love. Although my son is part of my call in life, so my work seems to be, too.

Please help my children to feel my love. Even more, help them to know Your love. I know that they understand that my love is a never-coming-and-going love. Help me not to worry. Help me, too, to discern when one of them does need me more than my work does.

So many children around the world are crying because adults are leaving them. So many adults cry because they are having to leave children. May we adults find ways to care for each other and our children, as we share our responsibilities and help our children grow. Amen.

A Prayer While in a Committee Meeting

Spokesperson God:

Why don't they speak up?
They see unfairness.
They question.
Why leave it to me?
Are You speaking, doing Your part?
Am I hearing You or my own arguments?

Ongoing Creation

Creating Spirit:

> *Our child, so precious a creation.*
> *Awesome; thank you, Creator.*
> *He lies there breathing, sleeping, dreaming his*
> *   own life.*
> *May I today in this life stage give birth anew*
> *   to what needs to be created in me,*
> *   released by me.*
> *So that it, too, can have a life of its own.*

AFFILIATION

Even in a culture which places a high premium upon independence and self-fulfillment, it is obvious that we long to be with one another. "I want somebody to love," is the theme of pop music in every generation. Whether we are in pain or in a joyous mood, most often we want to be with others. Children run to be held when they skin their knees. Adults fly across the country to be with relatives who are having surgery. When we play a game, reach a goal, have a birthday, we want to celebrate with others.

At each life stage being with someone is a crucial need. The infant must be with a nurturer, must be touched, to survive physically as well as emotionally and spiritually. Many children at very early ages begin to beg their parents to let them invite their friends over. Teenagers spend hours on the phone talking with their best friends. We spend much of early adulthood focusing upon whether and whom we will marry. As a person approaches middle age he or she becomes more involved affiliating with younger generations, nurturing them and the world into which they will grow. A challenge for older adults is how to maintain relationships and intimacy amidst changes and the death of loved ones.

Judaism and Christianity are communal religions. No one can be genuinely religious alone. Each of us shares, worships, works and rejoices with others. Our faith traditions encourage us to celebrate the crucial moments of affiliation with our church or synagogue.

The child is baptized or brought into the covenant of Abraham, in recognition of her or his affiliation with the faith community. Weddings celebrate the bond of affiliation between two individuals. At funerals we mourn the fact that the beloved is no longer with us.

We have a similar need to be with the Deity. The events of the Christian liturgical year reiterate again and again that we are with the Deity. During Advent we celebrate the coming of Christ into the world. God is coming to be with us in the presence of Christ. Jesus is born and called Immanuel, literally, "God is with us." Jesus' predominant message throughout his ministry was precisely that: God is here now; the Kingdom of God is at hand. We celebrate Epiphany, the coming of the Wise Men to the Christ at Bethlehem. Epiphany means that God appears, is manifested, is with us. The Resurrection celebrates the restoring of our relationship with God, through Christ, the Risen Lord. Even Pentecost focuses upon affiliation as it celebrates the presence of the Holy Spirit with the community of the faithful.

Virtually all prayers in groups or in private begin with the reminder that we are with God. We "invoke" the Spiritual Presence, acknowledging our desire for affiliation, whether we pray out of gratitude, in sorrow, to confess, to adore, or to ask. People pray, "Be with Susan as she goes through this time of trial"; "Be with Jonathan as he finds friends"; or "Be with the leaders of our countries as they negotiate disarmament." I have heard many grandparents pray for grandchildren with such words as, "God, be with them as they go on their trip." Some people bid friends farewell by saying, "Go with God," "Vaya con Dios."

These prayers are not worded to be for healing, for safety, or for peace, but rather ask simply that God be with these people. Our prayers are dominated with desire for reassurance of affiliation with God.

The need for withness is dominant in the following four prayers. In them, the way the Deity is thought of sets the tone for the emphasis upon the affiliative need.

Time Alone

Infinite Companion:

*Children right now are calling to You,
wondering what to do with their time alone. No one
to play with, afraid, bored, and also curious.*

*Adults are calling to You, asking for guidance
as they choose what to do with their time alone. For
some, time is a burden, a vessel to be filled up with
something, someone. For others, time alone is rich
and creative. For most, it is a mixture of fullness
and emptiness.*

*Couples, newly married and those celebrating
fiftieth anniversaries, are asking You, how much
time do they need to spend together, how much
alone? What is the right proportion? How can they
balance their differing needs of time alone, even
time alone with You, and time with each other.*

*Mothers, Fathers, Aunts, Uncles, and Grand-
parents who find themselves with children all day
long are asking for "five minutes peace" — an
evening would be heavenly.*

*When we have time alone, we often fear the
necessity to make choices of how to spend our
time. When we have no time alone, we crave the
opportunity to make that choice ourselves.*

*May we experience time as a blessing. May we
make the very best of our time — alone or with
others. Amen.*

With

Lightning and Thunder Maker:

*May I be held close by You,
to receive Your comfort until the storm is over.*

Single

Infinite Lover:

In the eyes of the world, I am "single." I live alone. But how far from "single" I feel! I am connected with my friends, my family, and those whom I care about around the world.

Joyous am I — when I realize I am quite free to make my decisions.

Lonely — sometimes. Ah, to have someone to exclaim to when I see a sunset like I saw tonight.

Unsure — whether the future will be one shared with another or lived by myself.

Hurt — when I get the one chair at the end of the table, or am not invited at all.

Relieved — when I think of the relationships I did not pursue, for they would not have been good.

May I live gracefully my individual existence. May I care for others even though they are not formally my "family." May I not become too self-centered or too walled-in from needing others. May I be open to friendships when they are ripe. May I be ready to join with another if that is right; may I have the wisdom to know if joining is not right.

Infinite Lover, You are with me. How can I ever be alone?

A Prayer to Befriend Others

Divine Friend:

I want You to befriend me, but then I know that You already do.
I guess I want to befriend You more consistently.
It is my initiative I need, not more of Yours;
You take initiative all the time.
I care deeply about the people of the world.
My sisters and brothers:

those who are starving and those who are studying;
those who are powerless and those who hold positions of great power;
those who are not free to talk — to spouses, colleagues, parents,
those who are not inwardly free to be silent;
those who have to walk to get water and those who sense no limits on Your resources;
those who mourn the loss of intimacy and those who long to know intimacy, even to lose it;
those who want to work and those who are workaholics;
those who are crossing borders, hoping for freedom and
those who are on the boundary — half in an institution, half out.

I want to befriend these people.
Somehow I feel I befriend them in an underground way when I combine the thought of them with the thought of You. I want also to act openly in ways which will help, and I need Your guidance in how to do that. Amen.

There are times when a person will be most aware of one spiritual need or the other: a woman making a major decision longs to be wise, *like* Divine Wisdom; a man experiencing grief longs to be *with* an Infinite Friend. At times now I begin a prayer with "Author" to help myself identify with God's creative power through the use of words. When I was lonely for a period of time, I stressed the fact that I was with the Deity by beginning my prayers with "Infinite Friend." But both spiritual needs — to be "like" and "with" the Infinite Companion — need to be met.

An African-American clergywoman had served her local church for one year when she told a small gathering of clergywomen of her exhaustion. Some members of her congregation had become so dependent upon her care that she often felt like she was a "mama" to many of these people. She said that she had felt a painful need for a Mama to lean on. Then she remembered. She had one — a Divine Mama — she could name, pray to, and lean upon for support. *Likeness* to the Divine image of Mama enhanced her awareness that she was *with* that very Presence.

UNEVEN DEVELOPMENT OF THE SPIRITUAL NEEDS

The prayers in this chapter have begun with these images of the Deity: Black God, Father in Heaven, Mother God, Creating Spirit, Spokesperson God, Infinite Companion, Lightning and Thunder Maker, Infinite Lover, and Divine Friend. If that array of images were used when we pray, beginning when we were very young, we would gradually sense that we are in some ways made in the image of the Deity, and we would come to trust that we are with that Deity. Optimally, all people would have the opportunity to fulfill the twin spiritual needs. But because virtually all the metaphors named, all the images drawn, and all the voices portrayed for the Deity have been male and white, females and people of color have been less able to experience themselves as being "like" God. Meanwhile, males do not develop their capacity to affiliate with the Deity as fully as they might because they have only powerful and parental male images of the Deity with which to relate in prayer.

There is an uneven development of these spiritual needs for both males and females. Neither can fulfill their spiritual dimensions or all aspects of their personalities adequately.

The same message is presented to females and males: Depend upon God. Even though God and humans are interdependent, the half of interdependence which focuses upon human responsibility has not been stressed. Not only do the dominant metaphors used for the Deity (Almighty God, Father, Lord) reinforce dependence rather than interdependence, they are masculine.

Women in our culture have been encouraged to be dependent upon men, and they hear this message to depend upon God. It is easy, then, for females to affiliate with God by overemphasizing dependency upon a powerful Divine Male. Simultaneously women lack the empowerment to be gained from sensing ourselves as genuinely being made in God's likeness. We can identify with some qualities of the Deity, even if God is given masculine names, voice, and images, but that identification is limited. Women have been identifying with the nurturing qualities of the Deity, but not with the name or power of that very Deity.

It is easy for males (who have been encouraged culturally to underemphasize affiliations in general) to underdevelop their affiliation with the Deity. Dependency of woman on father is more acknowledged and acceptable in our culture than dependency of man on father. Men do not as readily acknowledge their need for being with their Divine Father as women do. But men can feel that they are made in the image of God.

Women need to have the opportunity to know that they are made in the image of the Deity, and they need to stretch their affiliation with the Deity to include interdependent functions, not just dependent ones. Men need a healthier affiliation with the Deity (seen as feminine as well as masculine) and to wean themselves from any overidentification with qualities of the Deity which have been too attached to males (such as power and dominion). Both males and females suffer from the exclusive use of masculine metaphors for the Deity which suggest dependency upon an all-powerful being. Both would benefit from diverse metaphors for the Deity and from more metaphors which would suggest interdependency.

Let us look at how metaphors could help. For a long time females have depended upon God the Father; they do not identify with Father. Males do not sense their interaction with God the Father as much, but do identify with Him. If Colleague, Co-Worker, Friend, and Beloved were used when we spoke and prayed with the Deity, then females would affiliate with the Deity in an interdependent way, and they would be able to identify more meaningfully with the god-like qualities which they possess. Males could be encouraged to think of themselves in a more affiliative relationship with the Deity, their Colleague, Friend, Beloved, and Co-Worker, yet they could still identify with those very metaphors.

Likewise, the more colorful our metaphors for the Deity are, the more people of color will sense themselves to be made in the image of the Deity and the more whites will balance their identification with the Deity with a healthier affiliation with the Deity, a Deity whose image is not only white, but also colorful.

Blacks have identified to a limited extent with white pictures of Jesus, but when a black person hears of or sees a Black Jesus, there stirs far deeper emotional and behavioral ties. Males would not automatically be cut off from identification with the Divine if the Deity were named occasionally with feminine images; they could even identify in ways which they had not been able to before. And white people would have opened up for them new vistas as they think of the Deity in colorful ways.

The needs to be with and like the image of the Deity are natural for all of us. Most of the time we do not think about these needs; we just use what images we are given and stumble upon meaningful ones along our life's journey. Some of us find the given images to be inadequate, so we search intentionally. If we have been relatively content with our Divine images, it almost invariably hurts to be informed that others are hurting when they use the very metaphors for the Deity which have been meaningful for us. It is precisely because our Intimate Friend is so intimate that we are attached to how we name It. We often fear just contemplating change. If we decide to expand our images for the Deity, the search is sure to include some pain — but there is much promise for a profound encounter with the Power which is beyond any image or name.

FOR REFLECTION AND ACTION

1. With whom have you identified during your life, from childhood to your present age? List various people who, whether
   they knew it or not, affected you in that you "tried on"
   a behavior or attitude of theirs, seeking to be like them in
   some way.

2. Consider ways in which you think that you are made in the
   image of the Deity, finite ways in which you have qualities or
   capacities which are similar to God's, though God's capacities
   are infinite.

3. Reflect upon times you have been very close to someone,
   times when your sense of being with the other was or is
   very strong.
      Recollect times and situations which foster your sense of
   being very much with the Deity. See whether you can detect
   what prevents you from feeling close to another person or
   prevents you from feeling close to the Deity.

4. Over a period of time — perhaps a week — write out several
   prayers or speak them into a tape recorder.
      Review how you prayed, noting when you felt most
   "with" the Deity and when you were focusing on your
   "likeness" to God's image. Look for other spiritual needs
   which you were seeking to meet in your praying.

5. List several ways you see yourself (e.g., father, teacher, picker-
   upper, peacemaker, introvert).
      Now consider these descriptions of yourself as aspects
   of the Deity. Which are laughable, not applicable at all?
   Which have a fascinating affinity to how you believe the Deity
   to act or be?

Chapter Three

METAPHORS GALORE:

Hundreds of Names
for the Deity

Enspirited

Holy Breath:

As I take a deep breath I feel Your presence, enlivening me, refreshing me, giving me sustenance and new life.

You breathe through me lightness where there is heaviness. May I let the weight go.

You breathe through me peace where there is turmoil. May I be peaceful.

You blow insights my way. May I see, hear, and act.

You twirl chaos into order, if I wait long enough — may I be patient.

You create whirlwinds out of my neat and tidy life. May I trust what You are doing.

You are so quiet at times that I cannot be sure that You are there.

May I keep listening.

As I take a deep breath I feel Your presence, enlivening me, refreshing me, giving me sustenance and new life. Amen.

An East Ohio couple who enjoy sailing discovered that when they pray, "Anchor," "Wind," and "Compass" are meaningful metaphors for God. They are confident in their boat with their finite anchor, compass, and natural wind. Because nautical images are so poignant for them, thinking of God metaphorically as Anchor, Wind, and Compass evokes trust in prayer as well. Others have found meaningful metaphors for their prayers. One young woman wrote, "Good friends cannot always be there for us. The Divine Friend has no such limitations."[1] Another, a student, prayed, "God, My Mentor, My guide, teach me!"

Some have argued that the question of how to name the Deity is not the concern in prayer that it is in speaking and writing. This argument suggests that in prayer we can simply speak in the second person, with "You," "Thou," or "Thee." Yet, even if we do not name the Deity with a metaphorical image as we pray, we nevertheless have an image in the recesses of our unconscious, for we have developed and strengthened our images through hearing and reading. The metaphors used in speaking and writing have become those silent authoritative metaphors which inform our praying.

We inhabit a world filled with imagery; we need imagery. Our images must be made conscious — even more conscious — or that which is unconscious will continue to rule us without our acknowledgment or choice.

METAPHORS
WHAT THEY ARE AND ARE NOT

A metaphor is used to imply a likeness between two things. When we speak of having a sky-blue sweater, we mean that the color is very much like that of the sky. But we realize just as we say it that the color is not exactly like that of the sky. For one thing, the texture of the sweater does not match the smoothness of a blue sky. For another thing the sky changes color at different times of day and in different seasons. We understand that we are using a metaphor — that the sweater is sky-blue in one sense but is not actually the color of sky. A metaphor which seeks to describe one object by associating it with another evokes our response, "It is like that!" but also our echoing awareness, "It is not like that!"

Theologian Sallie McFague has helped to remind us that the names we use for the Deity are metaphors. She has pointed out that if we do not keep in mind both the "it is" and the "it is not" quality of the metaphor, then we lapse into either irrelevancy or idolatry. As long as there is an "it is," a likeness perceived, the metaphor can be relevant. But unless there is the "it is not," the difference recognized, the metaphor becomes an idol, mistaken for the Deity itself.[2]

If you can visualize a Mother Hen (Matthew 23:37, Luke 13:34), see her pulling her chicks under her wings, and sense some of that feeling in relationship to God, then "Mother Hen" is relevant for a God metaphor. If you have no idea what a mother hen is or cannot grasp the caring quality of that metaphor, the "it is" quality is gone; the metaphor is not viable. On the other hand, if you tend to see God only as Mother Hen, then you have made an idol of that metaphor. You have forgotten that the Deity is also not like a mother hen.

Of course it is very difficult to forget the "it is not" aspect of a metaphor like Mother Hen, for this metaphor does not enjoy society's dominant underscoring. Idols are generally made with cultural support, for the idol begins to be seen by many as reality, rather than a metaphor for that reality.

Two metaphors which have been used for the Deity are Lord and Seamstress. The Deity is like a Lord in certain ways: The Deity oversees; there is protective responsibility to offer guidance; the Deity provides for, cares; there is power and authority in the Deity. To say that the Deity is Lord is to lift up these overseeing, protective, provider, and authoritative qualities. Lord is one apt metaphor for the Deity. But, as is true of all metaphors, there is not just likeness intended, but also a striking dissimilarity between the two objects of the comparison. The Deity is not like a Lord in certain ways: The Deity is not just over, but also under and through; the Deity is not a human person; God is not just a powerful protector, but also a servant — one who responds to our actions.

The Deity is like a Seamstress (Genesis 3:21) in certain ways: God sews goals and guidance into our lives, helping to create us, and God measures us anew each time God creates for us. But the Deity is also not like a Seamstress: God is not a human person and does not fashion us without our cooperation. We are not fabric, without a will of our own; the Deity is not the only creator, since we, too, create. With any metaphor which we use for the Deity in prayer, we need to be able to affirm: The Deity is and the Deity is not like this.

Theologian Nelle Morton spoke of metaphors as shattering the inadequate image a person has outgrown and ushering in a new reality. The shock in hearing the metaphor comes first. Then gradually the likeness referred to by the metaphor is realized. A new horizon has been opened up because of the shattering and the opening.[3] When you first hear Mother Hen as a metaphor for the Deity, you may be surprised; there is a striking dissimilarity between the Deity and a mother hen! Then there is an opening, a tender connection between the caring of the hen with her own wings and the caring of the Deity. The Deity has taken on new meaning by the use of that metaphor, and, of course, so have mother hens.

Another guideline which assists us in recognizing the relativity of metaphors for the Deity is to think of God "as" rather than "is." "Rather than claiming God *is* Black or God *is* Father," Jenny Yates Hammett suggests that we "make clear our symbolic intent and speak of God *as* Father or God *as* Mother."[4] God *as* an Eagle lifts me to new heights; God *as* the Depth of Being connects me with all that is; God *as* Author taps my sense of creativity through words; the Divine *as* Womb taps that same creativity, but leads me to trust my own physical creativity. God *is* not a bird, *is* not down more than up, *is* not any profession, and *is* not so physical as to be or to have a womb.

A wise family therapist says that a family member "shows laziness," rather than "is" lazy or "acts bossy" rather than "is bossy." The use of language to demonstrate only what the therapist is currently seeing implies that the behavior or attitude could be different at another time. The therapist avoids "labeling" a person, partly to enable the person to sense her or his freedom to change and partly to increase the family members' expectations for that individual.[5] Likewise, we can think of the Deity as showing Love, the Deity as evidencing Comfort, as demonstrating Challenge, as behaving like a Sister, or as seeming to be Silent. This way of naming the Holy One implies that we expect to experience the Divine in other ways in the future. God is capable of demonstrating many qualities — we are open to the revelation of God through an array of possibilities.

I am using the terms "metaphor," "image," and "name" for the Deity rather interchangeably. Strictly speaking, metaphor is the most accurate because what I am talking about is a provocative label for some aspect of the Deity which evokes the response in us: "God is like that," and the echoing phrase, "but of course God is also not like that." Each word on the list in this chapter is a metaphor. The ones which are concrete, like Anchor, are more easily thought to be metaphors. But abstract words like "The Holy One" and "Eternal Presence" are metaphors, too. God is like one who is holy and like a presence which is eternal. But, God is not, for God is even more than holy and more than eternal. The word "image" implies that we actually visualize the Deity in some way. We do tend to associate an image with a metaphor, and sometimes we will want to do that quite intentionally. But we can use a metaphor without a clear "image" of it.

"Names" for God would more accurately be called "nick-names" — ways we call the Deity, knowing that we are not using a "real" name. It is impossible to think of any name which is not a metaphor and does not conjure up some image. Some people believe they hold no image whatsoever for the word "God." Yet, clearly "God" does have some associations because if the pronoun *It* is used to refer to the name, many people become upset that a "personal" dimension seems to be lost.

HUNDREDS OF METAPHORS FOR THE HOLY ONE

In this section there is a long list of metaphors for the Deity. The list can never be "complete," for there is no limit to the ways we can name what cannot accurately be described with any name. It may seem foolish to provide a list; I could simply say, "choose vital, relevant metaphors." But when we are not given suggestions, we tend to have difficulty coming up with ideas. When ten metaphors are provided, we can think of three more. When fifty are offered, we find ten or fifteen more; when a hundred are given, even more come to mind. This list is intended to function as a "priming of the pump," to get the reader to start imagining what would be poignant at this moment in her or his life or in the life of her or his community.

The list of metaphors is presented in five categories: Gender-Free, Feminine, Masculine, Feminine or Masculine, and Gender-Full. I believe that most of us would gain the most spiritual and psychological growth — and be most true to the nature of the Divine — if we used metaphors from each category throughout our lives. Using metaphors in each category in public worship reaches people who have varying affinities, challenges those who have diverse resistances, and testifies to a theology which affirms that the Deity is known in diverse ways.

I offer suggestions from both contemporary usages and from past resources. Biblical references are noted beside metaphors which were either used or alluded to in the Bible, although no attempt is made here to secure all the references for each of these metaphors. Because the translations vary, you may find that the Bible you consult does not contain the name listed; the translation you are using may only allude to the name listed.

The fact that a metaphor has been used in the Judeo-Christian tradition often gives people permission to use it. However, as we begin to experiment with the use of different metaphors in our prayers, a particular metaphor's meaningfulness to us will likely become the primary reason for choosing it — rather than its familiarity or prior use.

This list is limited by my own experience and language. I offer it here in the knowledge of its limitations. We need to think inclusively of color, culture, and ethnicity when we think of the Deity, or we fall into idolatry — thinking of the Deity only "like" one set of people and not "like" others as well. We need people of many cultures to brainstorm such lists.

GENDER-FREE OPTIONS

The Gender-Free options are metaphors which have no human analogue; therefore, there is no gender reference. These metaphors are likely to create the least inner struggle as new metaphors. They are definitely perceived as the "safest" to use in public. They seldom cause alienation in a hearer and seem inclusive. However, for deeper

identification and affiliation, we really need the more personal images. The ones which are feminine or masculine need to
supplement these gender-free options.

Absence
Aim
All[6]
All-powerful God* or Powerful
    God (Ps 147:5)
Almighty God (Job 5:17)
Anchor (Heb 6:19)
Answer to all Mysteries*
Awesome God* (Deut 7:21;
    Neh 1:5, 9:32)
Being Itself
Beyondness
Binder of Wounds* (Ezek
    34:16, Hos 6:1, Ps 147:3)
        Wounder (Job 5:18)
Black God
Breath of God (Job 27:3,
    33:4; Is 30:33, 40:7)
Brokenness
        God as one who breaks
        (Ezek 30:21-22)
Burden-lifting God (Ps 55:22,
    81:6; Mt 11:28-30)
Ceaseless Working[7] (Lam
    3:22, Is 40:28)
Comfort of Sufferers*
    (Ps 119:50, 76; Is 51:12;
    2 Thess 2:16)
Compass
Creating God (Gen 1:1, 26)
Creative and Nurturing God
Creative Source of all being*
    (Heb 11:3)
Creator (Gen 1, 2, Is 40:28,
    Rom 1:25, Rev 4:11)
Creator and Preserver of
    Allkind*
Cry (The Cry)[8]
Cycles

Darkness
Deity (Acts 17:29)
Divine Ally
Divine Being
Divine Process
Divine Spirit
Emptiness
Eternal One (Deut 33:27,
    Rom 16:26)
Eternal Presence
Eternal Source of Comfort
    (2 Thess 2:16-17)
Existence Itself
Ever-Living God* (Ps 9:7)
Ever-Loving God* (Ps 136)
Faithful God* (I Cor 1:9,
    10:13)
First and Last* (Is 44:6,
    Rev 22:13)
Fountain, Water of Life
    (Jer 17:13, Rev 21:6)
Generous Provider of All
    Good Gifts* (1 Cor 2:12)
Giver of Life (Job 33:4)
Giver of Light
Giver of Peace
God
God of All Colors
God of the Covenant (Gen
    9:17, Ezek 16:62, Lk 22:20)
God of gods (Deut 10:17)
God of Israel (Ex 5:1, 2 Sam
    23:3, 2 Kings 10:31)
God of Life and Death
God of Peace (Rom 15:33,
    16:20; Phil 4:9)
Gracious Giver of knowledge*
    (Prov 2:6, Eccles 2:26,
    James 1:5)

*From a list entitled "Names, Titles, Phrases Applied to God (non-sexist)" which
was compiled by Davelyn Vignaud and distributed by the Board of Discipleship of
the United Methodist Church.

Gracious God* (Jonah 4:2)
Great God (of power)* (Deut
    7:21, 9:29; Ps 66:3)
Great God our Hope*
    (Jer 14:8, Ps 71:5)
Ground of Being
Heart's Delight* (Is 58:14,
    Ps 37:4)
Hidden God*
High and Holy One* (Is 57:15)
Holy One (Lev 19:2, 1 Pet
    1:16)
Holy One-in-Three (Jn 14:26)
Holy Spirit (Mk 1:10, Jn 14:26)
I Am; I Will Be What I Will Be;
    I Will Cause to Be What I
    Will Cause to Be
    (Ex 3:13-14)
Incognito God* (i.e., Moses
    with the Burning Bush,
    Ex 3:2-6)
Infinite Challenger
Infinite God*
Inspiration to Goodness*
Isness
It[9]
Keeper (Ps 121:5)
Knowing One
Liberator (Is 49:9, 61:1;
    Lk 4:18-19)
Life-giver (Job 33:4;
    Ps 119:154, 156;
    1 Tim 6:13)
Light (Ps 27:1, Is 60:20,
    Jn 1:5)
Logos (The Word) (Jn 1)
Love (1 Jn 4:8)
Maker of all Things
Maker of Heaven and Earth*
    (Gen 14:19, 22)
Merciful God (Deut 4:31,
    Neh 9:31)
Mighty God* (Deut 10:17,
    Is 9:6, Jer 32:18)
Mighty Rock (Ps 62:2, 7;
    89:26)
Mind of the Universe*
Most High, or God Most High
    (Gen 14:18, Deut 32:8, and
    in many Psalms)
Nothingness
Nurturer

One Who is Always There
Our Beginning and Our End*
    (Rev 1:8, 21:6, 22:13)
Our Refuge and Our
    Strength* (Ps 46:1, 62:8)
Overhanging Tree
Peacemaker
Power of Being
Power that Saves* (Ps 67:2,
    78:22)
Presence
Proclaimer of Justice* (Is 42,
    Mt 12:18)
Puzzle, Puzzler
Radiant, Glorious God
    (Ps 76:4)
Rainbow God
Rebel
Reconciler (Col 1:20,
    2 Cor 5:18)
Redeemer (Job 19:25; Ps
    19:14; Is 47:4, 60:16)
Refuge (Deut 33:27, 2 Sam
    22:33, Ps 31:2)
Rhythm (Divine Rhythm)
Righteous God* (Ps 71:19,
    112:4; Dan 9:14; Is 45:21;
    1 Jn 2:1)
Rock (Gen 49:24, Deut 32:15,
    2 Sam 22:2-3)
Sacred and Intimate One
Searcher of Hearts*
    (Ps 139:1, 1 Chron 28:9,
    Rom 8:27, Rev 2:23)
Shelter from the Storm*
    (Is 25:4)
Shield (Gen 15:1; 2 Sam
    22:31; Ps 18:30, 28:7)
Shining Glory*
Silence
Singer of New Songs
Song (Ex 15:2)
Source of Blessing, Creation,
    Freedom, Life, Mercy,
    Peace...*
Sovereign God* (1 Tim 6:15)
Spirit (Mk 1:10, Jn 4:24)
Spirit of God, see Wind of
    God (Gen 1:2, Ex 31:3,
    Lk 4:18, Mt 3:16)
Spirit of Life
Spirit of Peace

Spirit Within
Spiritual Presence
Steadfast and Loving One*
    (Lam 3:22; 2 Chron 7:6;
    Ps 17:7, 48:9)
Strength (Ex 15:2; Ps 18:1,
    28:7)
Strength of the Weak*
    (Is 35:3, Ezek 34:16,
    Lk 1:51-55)
Supreme Intelligence
Supreme Reality
Surprising One
Sustainer (Ps 55:22,
    1 Cor 1:8)
Technicolor God[10]
Thou
To Be[11]
Total Mystery
True Light (Jn 1:9)
Trustworthy One (Ps 111:7)
Truth

Ultimate One
Understanding God
    (Ps 147:5)
Unity of All Life
Unobtainable
Upholder of the Falling*
Watchful and Caring God*
    (Gen 31:49-50, Jer 1:12)
Water
Way (Jn 14:6)
Wind
Wind of God (*Ruach,* a
    feminine word in Hebrew)
    see Spirit of God
    (Gen 1:2)
Wisdom (Prov 3, 8 and many
    others; 1 Cor 2:6-8)
    Spirit of Wisdom (Is 11:2)
Wise God (Rom 16:27)
Wondrous Fashioner and
    Sustainer of Life*
Word (Jn 1:1)
You

Even this long list does not encompass all of the possibilities for Divine metaphors. For example, many animals and birds are used in the Bible as metaphors which emphasize a certain quality of God: "God is like an eagle, stirring up its nest..." (Deuteronomy 32:11); "I am like a moth...like a lion..." (Hosea 5:12, 14).

When the Deity is referred to by such metaphors as Nothingness, Emptiness, Darkness, Brokenness, Absence, Clown, or Rebel, it is the experience of the believer which is being emphasized. God seems like Emptiness at times. Those who have experienced a period of time in which their relationship to the Deity was very confusing will likely find some of these choices meaningful, but these metaphors can be of value to most of us at some time. Certainly many in our biblical tradition have felt God to be absent and perplexing at times — and have told God so. Here are three examples of prayers which are framed around Gender-free metaphors for the Deity.

On Ending the Day with More Things to Do

Giver of Time:

Surely I am not requested by You to do more than I can.

May I coordinate my hats (roles), purses (finances), pens (work), crayons (play), and computers (details).

May I enjoy each task, while it is occurring.

May I discern what to prune out of my life.

Forgive me for living for my children's bedtime, living for the end of the school semester, and living for the completion of a book.

Thank you for Your flexibility; may I accept it gracefully.

Aim for Healing; Accepting Limitations

Spirit of Being:

Shall I accept my limitations or aim for healing?

Shall I accept my limitations or aim for healing?

Shall I accept my limitations or aim for healing?

Which limit? How much healing?

Fill in my gaps of knowing.

May I understand whatever I need to understand to cooperate with Your healing process and to prepare myself to live with any necessary limits.

May I accept gracefully the limits which I must, but reject what could be transformed into something better.

Help me, please, to use discernment, but not to feel it's all up to me.

I am not alone.

Help me with Your healing and loving presence.

Amen.

Control

Powerful Challenger:

> *I can't make my children sleep or eat.*
> *I don't know how my spouse will act.*
> *I don't even know how to control my own body.*

> *God, I want you to make clear to me what I need to control.*
> *You seldom make anything clear. FUZZY GOD.*

> *But I want guidance, Your guidance.*
> *Am I to be "out-of-control?"*
> *Or can I let go of control, without being "out of" it?*

> *You are not in control!*
> *You want, long, give, persuade, wait, whisper, and nudge.*
> *You act in love, but you depend upon us to respond.*

> *I will want, long, give, persuade, and wait.*

> *I will act in love, too — love for myself, my family, and our world — and depend on You to respond.*
> *A powerful thank you.*

FEMININE OPTIONS

For some time now, the greatest discussion regarding feminine metaphors for the Deity has been over the usage of the term "Goddess." Goddess is not a term which enjoyed acceptable usage in the Jewish or Christian past, partly because those religions which were competing with ancient Judaism and early Christianity in the same environment used a good deal of Goddess imagery, along with other ways of conceiving of the Deity. The Goddesses of competing religions were mentioned often in the Old Testament, as the

Hebrew tradition insisted upon the use of the Yahweh metaphor to the exclusion of others. In his missionary efforts as recorded in Acts, Paul competed with those who worshiped Goddess in Asia.[12] Although Christianity has often incorporated aspects of culture and philosophy which it found in its surroundings, the Goddess metaphor was not accepted by those who stabilized the canon nor by the church "fathers."

Jews and Christians found other ways throughout history to identify what they experienced to be feminine qualities in the Deity. The primary example for Christians is Mary, who played — and still plays — a crucial role as a feminine image to be addressed in prayer. "Mother of God" and the title officially given to her much later, "Queen of Heaven," (in 1950) had been ancient titles for Goddess.[13]

In Hebrew, the feminine Shekinah means the Glory of the Presence of God. Shekinah, Wisdom, and Spirit *(ruach)* were personified feminine motifs associated with the Divine which were available to the people of biblical times to balance the masculine imagery for God. Sophia, appearing in the Hebrew Scriptures as Creator, Wisdom, Teacher, Lover, and Tree or Plant, "symbolizes connectedness on a number of levels."[14] Once you become aware of these feminine personifications and motifs, it is surprising to see how often they occur in the Scriptures and how hidden they have become for most modern Jews and Christians.[15]

Bakerwoman God
Birther
Challenging Mother
Christ the Mother[16]
Comforting Mother
    (Is 66:10-13)
Divine Mother[17]
God of the Breasts
    (El Shaddai)[18]
Goddess[19]
Goddess of All Colors
Grandmother God
Lady Wisdom
Mama
Midwife (Ps 22:9-11, 71:6;
    Is 66:9)
Mother (Deut 32:18; Is 42:14,
    46:3, 66:13; Hos 11:3)

Mother-God
Mother Goddess
Mother Hen (or bird protecting
    young) (Deut 32:11-12,
    Is 31, Mt 23:37, Lk 13:34)
Mother of All[20]
Nursing Mother (Num 11:12,
    Is 49:15)
Seamstress (Gen 3:21)
Shekinah
Sister God
Sophia
Weaning Mother
Weaverwoman God
Womb (Is 46:3)
Womb Love[21]
Womb of God

"Mother" or "Goddess" function well as metaphoric images today because there is a vivid "It is" and "It is not" response. It is not likely that the metaphor "Goddess" would be thought of as reality rather than a metaphor for reality, because we do not tacitly assume that the Deity is female. The metaphor "God" is often taken to be the thing itself, not a metaphor for the Deity. So it is easy to make an idol out of the metaphor "God." There is often initial resistance when Goddess is named as a viable Christian metaphor for the Deity. At times people think that they are being asked to change the nature of the Deity or accept another deity alongside their old one. That is most definitely not the intent. We can use both words. Monotheism is a belief in one Deity, not a belief in one metaphor.

One day, when I was serving a local church, while driving from one pastoral visit to the next, I prayed regarding the conceiving of a child. I had prayed with "God" before about this longing. This time I gathered the courage to say "Goddess." (I had been introduced to this option about three years before, but had not found it relevant yet.) I said the name out loud several times, to increase my courage and to state boldly my claim to Her. I felt made in the image of Deity, and I felt that Divine Wisdom for my very female processes was somehow in touch with me. She had created so much — and I, in her image, was longing to carry on Her processes.

During the next three years, when I was pregnant twice, I sensed the power of Goddess beyond me and within me. Times when I felt insecure, afraid, or bubbling over with gratitude, I imagined — and almost felt — Her arms around me, embracing me and the new life inside me. She was giving birth through me, as I gave birth to my children. Nursing was not simple, either. I needed to learn how to coordinate my body's offerings with the hunger and security needs of our infants. Many times I cried and laughed with Goddess, as I felt She gave me strength and guided me through the uncertainties, exhaustion, and incredible joys of nursing. On a few occasions I even imagined nursing from Her; I so needed nourishment myself. (In fact, the Deity is alluded to as a nursing mother in Isaiah 49:15.)

I knew during these four and a half years of bodily mothering with two children that "God" would guide me. Intellectually I believed "God" was transcendent and immanent, beyond and within. "God" was beyond all, yet was very personal. But the name "Goddess" enabled me to identify with a feminine Wisdom and Presence. I experienced that Wisdom and that Presençe; I did not just believe in it. I could be "like" Her and "with" Her. "Goddess" meant to me theologically the same Presence that "God" had meant throughout my Christian upbringing. The new metaphor made the old Presence more vivid and vital for me. It was a personal choice, as all metaphors should be. "Goddess" will not appeal to all other people — even all other women. Nor do I assume that at every stage in my life the Goddess image will be as powerful as it has been these past few years, though it might be. It may become even more powerful as the ambiguities of parenting teenagers and the years of menopause approach. [22]

Lifetime Questioning

Eternal Sister:

> "*Everything Ends*"
> *I don't want to end.*
> *I want to live and live and live.*
> > *To live through the creation of children,*
> > *ideas, and work is satisfying.*
> > *But I want to live and live and live.*
> *Are monthly periods reminders of fertility and*
> > *potentiality, or limitations and*
> > *endings?*
> > *They began at 13 and will wane some day.*
> > *They swell me and change me and*
> > *occasionally pain me.*
> > *All are reminders of potentials — fulfilled*
> > *or unfulfilled.*
> *The moon lives and lives and lives.*
> > *I wouldn't mind waxing and waning if I*
> > *went on forever.*
> *But "everything ends."*
> *What goes on forever?*
> > *Do those I love?*
> > *Do I?*

MASCULINE OPTIONS

Masculine metaphors for the Deity are used consistently in the personal prayers of most contemporary Jews and Christians and in public worship. This list will look very familiar to us. Many adjectives could be combined with the name "Father" to create more options.

Adoptive Father (Rom 8:15, Gal 4:4-6)
Brother God
Challenging Father
Comforting Father (2 Thess 2:16-17)
Daddy (Abba) (Mk 14:36, Rom 8:15, Gal 4:6)
Divine Father
Everlasting Father (Is 9:6)
Father (Mt 26:39, Lk 11:2)
God (Jn 3:16)
Heavenly Father (Mt 6:26)
King (Ps 24:7, 47:7)
    King of kings (1 Tim 6:15, Rev 19:16)

Lord (Num 3:44, Ps 24:10, Lk 9:54)
Lord Almighty
Lord of Hosts (Jer 32:18)
Lord of Lords (1 Tim 6:15, Rev 19:16)
Lord of Peace (2 Thess 3:16)
Lord of the Dance
Loving Father (2 Thess 2:16,17)
Prince of Peace (Is 9:6)
Sovereign Lord (Rev 6:10)

The following prayers speak to the Deity in masculine images.

Peace

Prince of Peace:

May You walk gently upon this earth today.

May boys and girls who love to play with guns today be touched throughout their lives by Your Spirit, so that they grow up being as attracted to the majesty of peace as to the apparent power of war.

May these children witness today, in the people around them, POWER

as cooperation between neighbors,
as discipline to listen to one another,
as strength to control revengeful impulses.

Prince of Peace — May You walk gently upon this earth today.

Daddy

Comforting Daddy:

> *Your hand in our lives seems so big,*
> *Your voice, so powerful . . . when it's not stone*
> *quiet.*
> *To think of You with tears, sad for Your creation,*
> *is almost unbearable — easier to think of You*
> *dripping with sweat from Your untiring efforts.*
> *You play so rough (Why tornadoes,*
> *earthquakes, droughts?), rest so long (We wait),*
> *want so much (You're hardly ever satisfied, saying,*
> *"Next time, how about . . ."),and love so (Thanks for*
> *teaching us how to love).*
> *Do You ever feel alone? Do You know how*
> *much we love You?*
> *We take You for granted, but we need You so*
> *much.*

The Gift

Forgiving Father:

> *May I let go of my gnawing sense that You*
> *have not forgiven me. Gracefully You envision me*
> *anew. Please help me to let go of the chains of the*
> *past, to let the future be informed by, but not*
> *burdened by it. I accept Your gift. I accept Your*
> *forgiveness. Amen.*

OPTIONS WHICH EVOKE FEMININE OR MASCULINE IMAGES

Some metaphors, such as Father, clearly have a masculine reference, while others, such as Sister, refer to likeness with females. Yet there are many metaphors with human analogues which could evoke either masculine or feminine images in us. Whenever a human profession is lifted up as a metaphor for the Deity it is either a male or female in that profession which we think of as we name the Deity that way. We cannot think of the Deity as Physician or Nurse without also associating some gender to that Physician or Nurse, although the gender we associate with the metaphor of professions will vary at different times and is conditioned by cultural expectations.

Administrator of Life
Architect
Author
    Author of Life (Acts 3:15)
Baggage Carrier
Baker
Begetter
Beloved Friend
Blacksmith
Builder (Ps 127:1; Heb 3:4, 11:10)
Carpenter
Chef
Clown
Comforter (Is 66:13)
Companion of the Lonely*
Composer
Conductor
Counselor (Jn 14:26, 15:26)
    Wonderful Counselor (Is 9:6)
Dancer
Dentist
Designer
Divine Colleague
Divine Companion
Fashioner (Job 31:15, Ps 119:73)
Fixer
Friend (Jer 3:4)
Gardener
Glassblower
Guardian (1 Pet 2:25)
Guide
Healer of the sick* (Jer 30:17, Hos 11:3)

Helper*
    Helper of the fatherless (Ps 10:14)
    Helper of the helpless (Ps 10:14)
    Helper of the needy (Ps 72:12)
Judge
    Judge Eternal (Gen 18:25, Is 33:22, Heb 12:23)
Keeper of the Covenant
Keymaker
    Giving Keys (Mt 16:19)
    Holding Keys (Rev 1:18)
Knitter (Ps 139:13)
Liberator (The Exodus story, Is 61:1)
Life-giver (Job 33:4, 1 Tim 6:13)
Lover (Song of Solomon)
Lover of our Souls
Machinist
Master (Eph 6:9)
Master Builder, see Builder
Mechanic[23]
Mentor
Minister
Music Maker
Nurse
Nurturer
Overseer
Parent (Hos 11:3, 1 Jn 5:1)
Persuasive Friend
Physician

*From a list entitled "Names, Titles, Phrases Applied to God (non-sexist)" which was compiled by Davelyn Vignaud and distributed by the Board of Discipleship of the United Methodist Church.

Potter (Is 64:8)
Professor
Protector (Ps 68:5)
Provider (Gen 22:14,
  Ps 111:5)
Rabbi (Mt 23:8)
Rebel
Ruler (Is 33:22)
Savior (Is 60:16)
Servant
Sewer

Shepherd (Gen 49:24,
  Lk 15:3-7, 1 Pet 2:25)
Teacher (Is 30:20; Mt 12:38,
  23:8; Jn 13:13)
Tester
Thou (Ps 31:3)
Timekeeper
Time Manager
You (Ps 31:3, an example
  of many)

For a group celebrating communion, a metaphor which can be thought of as masculine or feminine is very helpful — for each participant can experience identification and affiliation privately, yet all share in the same metaphor.

Communion

Beloved:

> *One body. One Cup.*
> *One body, broken for us.*
> *One cup, a new covenant.*
Beloved, with whom we commune, are we faithful to
> *Your purpose? We recognize our brokenness;*
> *there are many reminders of that — broken*
> *relationships, broken hopes, broken bodies,*
> *broken dreams, broken faith. Have we also*
> *broken the covenant which was new two*
> *thousand years ago? We do not share our food*
> *enough. We do not care for one another as*
> *deeply as we might.*
May we, as we take this bread, acknowledge our
> *brokenness, but may we also acknowledge our*
> *healing and mending.*
May we, as we drink this juice, accept forgiveness for
> *having made the new covenant old to our*
> *practice, and may we accept it as new again,*
> *as we are renewed by it. Amen.*

Healing

Doctor of My Soul:

You Doctor and Nurse all creatures eternally. May You Doctor my doctors and Nurse my nurses into the right decisions as they help You to heal my body temple.

May I be receptive to You and to You in them. May I know when to speak to them, as I intuit Your guidance regarding my healing.

Thank You for Your many human hands, hearts, and eyes that care.

Shalom.

GENDER·FULL OPTIONS

Gender-full metaphors are those which refer to both masculine and feminine gender at the same time. Both genders are included either in one androgynous image or by imagining two or more persons in relation to each other.

Elohim is an important name for the Deity in the Old Testament. It is the name used in the first Genesis account of creation, Genesis 1:26, "And God (Elohim) said, 'Let us make humanity (Adam) in our own image, after our likeness. . .'"[24] Exactly what was meant by the plural Elohim is not known, for no description of the Deity appears, but Phyllis Trible, an Old Testament scholar, suggests that a hint of the Creator is given through the phrase "Image of God, male and female."[25] The plural name for God, Elohim, in whose image we were made, may have been used because God was seen as both male and female.

Christian theologians speak of the Trinity in part out of the need for thinking of the Deity in a variety of ways at the same time — creator, incarnate person, and active mover. The many metaphors which I list throughout this book can be seen as referring to various persons of the Trinity. For example "Holy Breath" may remind us of the Holy Spirit or make us think of the creating dimension of the Deity; precisely because the three are one, it can refer to any of the three "persons." The metaphor Trinity is itself a way in which the

Deity has been seen to be in relationship: The various aspects of the Trinity are in relation to each other. Often in Christian history all three of these "persons" were given masculine metaphors, but this was not always the case. Before the Christian Bible was formalized into its current state, a group of Christians who are called Gnostics used a number of descriptions of the Deity which alluded to both sexes in one image. The Divine Mother was characterized in three ways: as part of a Dyad (Mother-Father), as the Holy Spirit within the Trinity, or as Wisdom.

There were other gospels in addition to the four we know in the Christian Bible. In some of the gospels, which have been discovered at sites where these Gnostic groups worshipped, Jesus was said to have spoken of the Deity in feminine ways. In the *Gospel to the Hebrews* Jesus says, "my Mother, the Spirit." In the *Gospel of Thomas* Jesus again speaks of his divine Mother, the Holy Spirit, along with his divine Father — the Father of Truth. And, in the *Gospel of Philip* he says that whoever becomes a Christian gains "both father and mother" for the Spirit is "Mother of many." A vision of the Trinity is seen by John in the *Apocryphon of John:* "He said to me, 'John, Jo(h)n, why do you doubt, and why are you afraid?...I am the one who (is with you) always. I (am the Father); I am the Mother; I am the Son."[26]

Mystics, too, in all centuries have felt greater freedom than orthodox theologians in their use of metaphors, for their purpose was prayer, the experience of God, and they needed images full of gender to do that. Eleanor McLaughlin reminds us that medieval spirituality included a "minor but persistent and theologically responsible tradition which experiences God and especially Jesus as Mother and Sister as well as Father and Brother."[27]

One of the most well-known metaphors of medieval spirituality originated with the late fourteenth century mystical theologian Julian of Norwich: "Christ, My Mother." Speaking of Mother Jesus, she uttered such expressions as "My kind Mother, my gracious Mother, my most dear Mother, have mercy on me..."[28] Jewish mystics of the medieval Kabbala tradition spoke of the Divine Quaternity, which consisted of the Divine Mother and Father and the Son and Daughter.

In an effort to provide an image of the Deity which would evoke more "completion" or wholeness for Christians, psychologist Carl Jung in this century proposed feminine symbols for what he saw as a male-dominated set of symbols in Christianity. Among his suggestions was that a Quaternity be lifted up. A feminine aspect would be added to the Trinity to make it whole. Sophia would be a likely candidate, for She "was with God before time began and at the end of time will be reunited with God through the sacred marriage."[29]

Throughout this century Christian Scientists have named the Deity with the metaphor "Father-Mother God." This metaphor seems to have been used primarily to relay the motif of a Creator God which is not more like one parent than the other. However, a male-female relationship, lifted to a Divine metaphor in its expression as intimate friends rather than as parents, can present a model in which there is mutual support and understanding, cooperation rather than hierarchical power, and flexible role-interpretations for humans.

Beloved Couple	God/ess
Christ, the Mother	Infinite Couple
Divine Couple	Mother-Father God
Elohim	Trinity
Father-Mother God	Wise Couple

Rosemary Ruether is one of a number of users of the written word "God/ess." This term is the Divine corollary to the written inclusive pronoun for humans, "s/he." "S/he" is used to remind the reader that the person alluded to may be a female or a male. Just as "s/he" cannot be pronounced or used in oral speech, so too "God/ess" remains a written term, reminding the reader that the Deity is neither just God nor just Goddess. Ruether describes it "as a written symbol intended to combine both masculine and feminine forms of the divine while preserving the Judeo-Christian affirmation that divinity is one."[30] I include the term in the gender-full list in order to mention its existence and intent; however, it's usage in prayer is limited by the fact that it is heard as "Goddess," not "God/ess."

Challenges of Intimacy

Divine Couple,

For eternity You are in relation to each other. You must have answers for us, ways which will lead toward our understanding each other.

We love each other and think that we trust Your love. Please let us be open to Your Wisdom in our relationship.

I panic — think there's no hope we will resolve this crisis. Yet I sense we will. Guide me to really hear You, and guide him (her) to respond to You, too.

I hope that I am open. I think I want to know any ways I am closed to You or to him (her). Teach me. Thank you.

Grief over Death

Mother-Father God:

You have taught me much about life. Now I need to be taught about death. I have sadness, emptiness, a hole in my life. I know I can live without my loved one, but I do not want to have to.

I do not want to be too selfish. I know that this dear one had to live and die his life. But I was not ready. I guess I never would have been. I hope that he was ready, from Your perspective.

My prayer had been for him not to die until he felt very loved by all of us and by You. I am convinced that he did feel loved. I am grateful.

However You continue life beyond life as we know it; I trust You. You are gracious forever. But that does not heal the loss.

Thank you for the blessing of love shared between us. Thank you for maturity we learned through our problems, shared. Somehow through my tears I trust that in You he rests in peace and that in You all of us touched by him can also live in Your peace.

I do not understand, but I trust that Your peace does pass all understanding. Amen.

"Mommy, Mommy"

Mother-Father God:

"Mommy, Mommy" at home, in the middle of the
night, when the children cry.

"Father," "Father in Heaven," in church, when
people are awake, dressed up — where there is
status.

God, I can't call you "Father" — I'm angry.
Only "Mommy" strength gets me through. How dare
someone tell me that any name for God but "Father"
is an idol!

Please, Mother-Father God, help me sort all this out.

Dancing with God/ess

Dancing God
    dances through my body
        for flexibility,
        power,
        strength.
Dancing Goddess
    moves through my work
        as purpose,
        guidance,
        wisdom.
Dancing God
    twirls through relationships
        for freedom,
        responsibility,
        love.
Dancing Goddess
    flows through my life
        as joy,
        beauty
        value.

Looking at the long list of metaphors, you may feel immobilized by too many choices. You may have had a few familiar metaphors which you took for granted; now I am suggesting that you examine and consider using metaphors chosen from hundreds of ideas. In the next chapter I suggest issues to reflect upon in order to decide which particular metaphors are most valuable in a specific context.

When you anticipate expanding your use of metaphors for the Deity there is often a fear of loss. "My way of talking with God is precious to me. How can I change that?" There is frequently pain associated with the idea that you may eventually change or that others think that you "ought" to change. There is inertia — even when the change looks quite attractive. Often it is useful to announce any fear, pain, or excitement, to acknowledge it firmly to ourselves and perhaps to others.

We do risk the unknown when we try a new metaphor. After we choose and try out new metaphors for a while we can of course return to the ones with which we were familiar. But if we return to our original familiar metaphors for the Deity, we come back to them with a different view — we are now choosing them, not functioning out of habit. So even those old familiar metaphors will be revitalized.

FOR REFLECTION AND ACTION

1. Read the biblical passages listed below (or others which you choose), writing down metaphors which are used or implied in the reference to the Deity.

   a) Hosea 6:3
   b) Psalm 127:1
   c) Deuteronomy 32:11
   d) Lamentations 3:22

   e) Matthew 6:26 and 30
   f) John 12:46
   g) Isaiah 46:3-4

   How do you believe that the Deity is both "like" and "not like" each metaphor? (For example, in Isaiah 46:3-4 God is referred to as One who carries or bears, a Carrier or Bearer, as well as a Maker, Saver, or Savior. How is God "like" and "not like" a Carrier or Bearer?).

2. Does your own relationship with your human mother or father affect your use of the metaphors "Mother" and "Father" to refer to the Deity? If so, how?

3. With a sense of exploration, choose one name from each of the five categories (gender-free, feminine, masculine, feminine or masculine, and gender-full) to conceptualize the Deity as you pray five different times this week. Note your experience using various metaphors.

4. Choose a Psalm which is unfamiliar to you. Read it aloud. As you come to a name for God in the text, substitute for it a different one from the gender-free category (choosing quickly, without much deliberation). Notice the different meanings and connotations about the Deity which are suggested.

5. Listen to some people pray (e.g., yourself, a child, a minister). Make connections between the life experience of the person who prays and the way the Deity is named.

6. Choose a metaphor from one of the lists in this chapter which seems impossible for you to use in prayer. Try praying, using this metaphor, and observe your experience.

7. Return to the way you referred to the Deity, before exploring metaphors for God. Pray, using this old, familiar name. What is your experience now?

NOTES

1. Kathy Robothom, "Christian Prayer: Expanded Options" course, United Theological Seminary, Spring 1986.
2. Sallie McFague, *Metaphorical Theology: Models of God in Religious Language* (Philadelphia: Fortress Press, 1982) 1-29.
3. Nelle Morton, *The Journey is Home* (Boston: Beacon Press, 1985) 152-154.
4. Jenny Yates Hammett, *Woman's Transformation: A Psychological Theology* (New York: The Edwin Mellen Press, 1982) 13.
5. Peggy Papp, *The Process of Change* (New York: The Guilford Press, 1983) 8-9.

6. Starhawk, *The Spiral Dance: A Rebirth of the Ancient Religion of the Great Goddess.* (San Francisco: Harper and Row, 1979) 26-27.
7. Gordon E. Jackson, *Pastoral Care and Process Theology* (Washington, D.C.: University Press of America, 1981) 54.
8. John Cobb, Jr., *Liberal Christianity at the Crossroads* (Philadelphia: Westminster Press, 1972) 48, from Kazantzakis Report to Greco (New York: Simon and Schuster, 1965) 291-292.
9. Wolfgang Lederer, *The Fear of Women* (New York: Harcourt Brace Jovanovich, Inc., 1968) 157.
10. "Technicolor God" was used in the 1983 United Methodist Clergywomen's Consultation.
11. "Why indeed must 'God' be a noun? Why not a verb — the most active and dynamic of all?. . . isn't the Verb infinitely more personal than a mere static noun?" Mary Daly, *Beyond God the Father* (Boston: Beacon Press, 1973) 33.
12. Elizabeth Schussler Fiorenza, *In Memory of Her: A Feminist Theological Reconstruction of Christian Origins* (New York: Crossroads, 1983) 249.
13. Marina Warner, *Alone of All Her Sex.* (New York: Knopf, 1976) 65.
14. Susan Cady, Marian Ronan, Hal Taussig, *Sophia: The Future of Feminist Spirituality* (Retitled *Wisdom's Feast: Sophia in Study and Celebration,* 1989) (San Francisco: Harper and Row, 1986) 18-30, 75.
15. Leonard Swidler displays the various feminine images which are used in the Bible and in early Christian times in his book, *Biblical Affirmations of Women* (Philadelphia: Westminster, 1979).
16. Caroline Walker Bynum, Stevan Harrell, and Paula Richman (eds.), *Gender and Religion: On the Complexity of Symbols* (Boston: Beacon Press, 1986) 266-267.
17. Donald Gelpi, *The Divine Mother: a Trinitarian Theology of the Holy Spirit* (Lanham, MD: University Press of America, 1984).
18. *El Shaddai* is usually translated "the God of the mountains," but also means "the God of the breasts," Virginia Ramey Mollenkott, "Feminine Images of God in the Bible," *Circuit Rider,* June, 1982, 13, citing Phyllis Trible. Also Bro. Daniel F. Stramara, O.S.B., "El Shaddai: A Feminine Aspect of God," Dove Leaflet #28, November, 1985 (Pecos, NM: Dove Publications).
19. Linguistic analysis shows how the suffixes on words have changed to denote gender reference. In Old English the -er or -ere ending was a masculine suffix which referred to males only. The parallel usage for the female was -ster or -estre (as a "webster" was one who weaves, a "baxter" one who bakes, and a "seamster" one who sews). In Northern England men began to enter into these feminine professions, and the -ster suffix began to apply to males and females alike. A spinster, for example, referred to either a male or a female who spins. In Southern England the -ster suffix continued to refer primarily to women.
   Beginning with the Norman invasion in the eleventh century, the French influence introduced the suffix -ess, which began to be applied to women in particular, for example in "shepherdess" and "goddess." As -ster began to be used for males, the -ess ending became the more predominantly female referent.
   In the nineteenth century the Latin feminine ending -trix was used in a fashion similar to the earlier -ess, as in "obstetrix" (she who stands before to catch the baby). The suffix in the English language has changed gradually from a gender specific term to a neutral term. But, since males

are considered the norm, new feminine designations kept being introduced, until they, too, became neutral in meaning.

In contemporary usage the significance of the *-ess* suffix is not that it
identifies a female so much as it indicates a "deviation from what is
consciously and unconsciously considered the standard." This serves a
useful purpose when referring to Divinity, precisely to point out the
conscious intention.

For further explanation see Casey Miller and Kate Swift, *Words and
Women* (Garden City, NY: Doubleday, 1976) 47-50, 159.

20. Valentinus, a gnostic teacher and poet, assumed that God was essentially
    indescribable, but suggested that the divine could "be imagined as a dyad;
    consisting, in one part, of the Ineffable, the Depth, the Primal Father; and,
    in the other, of Grace, Silence, the Womb and 'Mother of All.'" Elaine
    Pagels, *The Gnostic Gospels* (New York: Random House, 1979) 50.
21. Phyllis Trible, *God and the Rhetoric of Sexuality* (Philadelphia: Fortress
    Press, 1978) 38.
22. Carol Christ discusses the value of the Goddess metaphor as an
    affirmation of the female body. "Why Women Need the Goddess:
    Phenomenological, Psychological, and Political Reflections," in Carol
    Christ and Judith Plaskow (eds.) *Womanspirit Rising* (San Francisco:
    Harper and Row, 1979).
23. Kay Short, a student at United Theological Seminary, noted that the
    metaphor "Mechanic" could stress the capacity of the Deity to bring
    "realignment." Spring, 1986.
24. Trible, op. cit., 13.
25. Ibid., 17-20.
26. Elaine Pagels, *The Gnostic Gospels* (New York: Random House, 1981)
    51-52.
27. Eleanor McLaughlin, "'Christ My Mother': Feminine Naming and Metaphor
    in Medieval Spirituality," *St. Luke's Journal of Theology* 18 (1975) 383.
28. As cited in Elizabeth Clark and Herbert Richardson, *Women and Religion:
    A Feminist Sourcebook of Christian Thought* (New York: Harper and
    Row, 1977), 112.
29. Carl Jung, *Answer to Job,* trans. R.F.C. Hull (New York: Bollingen
    Foundation, 1958, 1973) 85-86.
30. Rosemary Radford Ruether, *Sexism and God-Talk* (Boston: Beacon Press,
    1983) 45-46.

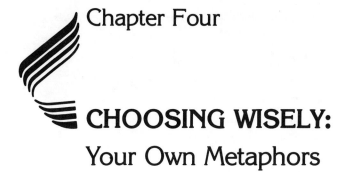

Chapter Four

CHOOSING WISELY:
Your Own Metaphors

Choosing

Choosy God:

I believe that You give us alternatives and expect us to choose. I realize our choices affect Your alternatives. Your choices affect our alternatives.

May I be guided in making the right choices today. May I choose how to think of You, how to name You, so that I might grasp Your presence in my life as fully as possible.

May I choose well how to live in my body, when to rest, work, play, and create.

May I choose with care what to say today.

May I choose wisely how to pray today.

May I be choosy when that matters, not accepting less than the best. But may I be accepting when acceptance matters more than doing the "best."

I feel chosen. We are all chosen, Your chosen. May we act as chosen, and as though all others, too, are chosen.

Thank You. Amen.

We need to develop healthy and responsible identification and affiliation with the Spiritual Presence — to sense that we are like and with God. I have argued that the consequences of the choices made, and made for us, have led females to be overly dependent upon a masculine imaged Deity and led males to overly identify with that Deity. Females have not had the opportunity to identify sufficiently while both females and males need to be challenged to affiliate with the Deity in more cooperative, interdependent ways.

I want to be clear that in choosing metaphors for the Deity we are not creating a Deity in an image which would help us psychologically. The Deity exists as It is — we will never know exactly what that Deity is like. An attempt has been made to describe the Deity by many throughout history. That discovery and naming process has never stopped and will never stop. We are participating in the same process as were the people of the Hebrew tradition and the early Christian tradition, when they looked at the Deity first this way, and then that way. But the numerous ways of thinking about the Deity have different effects upon us, and we do need to be aware of these effects. We cannot escape choosing metaphors; the point is to choose wisely.

When Jesus said, "Abba," he was saying what would now be understood by the English term "Daddy." Abba was a term which connoted familiarity; Jesus was proposing intimate language for the Deity. He needed to introduce new ways of naming God in order to elicit in his hearers the feeling of intimacy he wanted to convey. That is precisely what we are doing as we search for meaningful metaphors today. We are seeking to use metaphors which provoke the feelings and thoughts which are appropriate for our relationship to the Deity.

A woman who began to take seriously her choosing of Divine metaphors noticed that she had been saying "Lord" with every prayer in order to affirm the dominion of God. She tried various alternative metaphors and discovered that to begin a prayer with "Servant" altered her understanding of God positively. She realized that at that point in her life, she experienced God more often as servant than lord. Rather than feeling "below" God, as she had in saying "Lord," she began to feel God was with her — as a servant with her fellow sisters and brothers. There were times when "Lord" was appropriate, when the Servant seemed a Master. Together, this pair of metaphors forced her to think about her beliefs. Both servant-hood and lordship are Biblical motifs for the Deity; Christian theology holds the two images in tension. Yet, according to our experience and the purpose of the prayer, these two metaphors affect us quite differently.

Two key issues affect the identification and affiliation process, and reflection upon these two issues helps us to discern the possible effect of a metaphor or set of metaphors. First, how does the metaphor affect your self-respect? Second, what does the metaphor imply about power? I believe that the primary set of metaphors used by any individual should lead toward an enhancement in self-respect and an increased sense of cooperative power in relation to the empowering Deity — a relation that is interdependent.

The metaphors which we use in prayer in a given situation in our lives need to be compatible with saying "Because of the Deity, I have dignity" and "With the help of the Deity I can act responsibly because the Deity, I, and others depend upon one another." These statements are beliefs about humans. But they are also theological statements — they suggest that the Deity is One who is involved in ongoing creation, creating good beings who have the potential to make wise choices and who share power and responsibility with the Creator.

It is more likely that a person would arrive at a small cluster of vivid and valid metaphors than that she or he would find one metaphor which is always suitable. The woman who had used "Lord" expanded her options to include "Servant." In tandem, they triggered growth in her understanding of herself as a person of worth, with her own internal power, in an ongoing relationship with the Deity. I discover that if I pray to "Mother," I am likely to feel a deepened self respect and acceptance of myself; if I use "Teacher," I sense a cooperative power, God enabling me to gain internal power; when I pray "Sister," I feel intimacy and reciprocity. Also, it is possible that for some people a single metaphor, such as "Friend," would evoke equally valuable responses as a small cluster of metaphors does for others.[1]

SELF·RESPECT

Self-respect means a healthy regard for our dignity as well as the recognition of our obligations. Professor Hycel Taylor of Garret-Evangelical Seminary, speaking on the topic "Christian Spirituality from the Black Perspective," argued forcefully that all people need to feel that they are made in the image of God. If each of us could genuinely say, "I am made in the image of God and God said, 'It is good'" there would be healing on this earth, for individuals and communities.[2]

It is surely possible to think too highly of ourselves, to lean toward self-conceit. One of the best checks on this possibility is to ask ourselves whether we have a solid esteem for all other created beings, whether we can affirm that they, too, are made in the image of the Creator. Another check on the error of thinking too well of ourselves is to ask whether we truly sense God in our midst as the source of ongoing creation. For example, if we begin to take all the credit for bringing forth healing in a relationship, we may have forgotten that God is the source of healing power. God empowers us as we take responsibility for our own choices and recognize our obligations to others.

Male theologians such as Reinhold Niebuhr and Anders Nygren considered pride to be the sin of humans. Valerie Saivang pointed out in 1960 that although pride may have been the sin of men, the sin of many women was underdevelopment or negation of self.[3] Since self-respect includes both the healthy regard for one's dignity and the recognition of one's obligations, how we name the Deity affects both of these aspects of self-respect — the name needs to remind us who we are and what we must do. All too often the name used both publicly and privately for God in prayer reminds women of who we are not and what we cannot do. If the images I use are all quite different from anything I could ever be or do, I do not easily develop appropriate respect for myself as made in God's image. I will never be a father or a lord. I cannot be a son.

Males all too often miss being reminded of who they are not. If the images for the Deity are mostly male and virtually never female, a male easily and unintentionally senses that he, and especially he, is to be proud and to feel obligated for providing for all of creation.

Given the one-sided set of images, neither males nor females can have a healthy self-respect. Neither have themselves in perspective with the other or with the Deity.

When we consider the effect that using various metaphors has upon our self-respect, we might tend to choose some metaphors which definitely produce a feeling of "likeness," identification. But the question of self-respect ought also to lead us to include some metaphors in our repertoire which are different from us. We are reminded by those metaphors of the dignity of our brothers and sisters. The use of diverse metaphors functions to enhance the respect we have for others as well as for ourselves.

An important part of self-respect is the affirmation of our bodies. Women in our culture have a critical need to experience a deep acceptance of our bodies: their shape and sizes, their cycles and fluids, their physical needs as well as emotional and spiritual needs. While the Goddess metaphor affirms the female body in all of its stages, other feminine metaphors will evoke the affirmation of the body in particular stages. Womb of God, emphasizing birth, can be meaningful for a woman who is pregnant, but it also affirms the female body if it is used by a person who prays for birth in some other dimension of her or his life. The many ways of using the Mother metaphor in addressing the Deity evoke an affirmation of motherhood, including the mother's body. Women between puberty and menopause may find affinity and closeness with the Deity as Bleeding Goddess, one who can affirm the goodness of monthly bleeding, yet who can know the pain, worries, and ambiguities it evokes. People in several settings have informed me of the comfort they receive thinking of themselves or their loved ones rocked in the arms of a Grandmother God.

The divine metaphors in these prayers are compatible with the themes of personal dignity and worth, including obligations for others.

Accessibility

Accessible God:

Always accessible are You! No ramps, no hearing aids, no sign language is needed to reach you. You know our gifts and cherish each of us. Thank You.

Hurry to inspire us to be more accessible and caring, so that we may know one another's gifts and come to cherish each other. Thank You.

The Body as All Thumb

Wise Friend:

I recall that some wise friend said, "When the thumb hurts, the body is all thumb.'" So true. May I laugh at myself and accept Your laughter with me, for I have been "all me." I have been absorbed in myself, worried about myself.

May I now see beyond myself again, so that I care deeply and show my care for others. May I find ways, time, courage, and motivation to reach out. May I hear the pain of my child, not just my sense of nuisance. May I grasp the desires of someone who calls, their longings and needs, not just how those demands will fit into my schedule. May I be a world citizen, not preoccupied only with myself or nearby concerns.

I ask for forgiveness, and I know it is already given. You understood my worry over myself. I am precious, and that is all right to affirm. I am over my feeling sorry for myself, for now. Amen.

Loss of Potential

Loving and Wise Creator God:

*Like zucchini in a summer garden, You offer to
create more than I can nurture. Yet to say "No" to
Your potential creation is so painful.*

*How does one control the birth of too many
opportunities, of too many relationships, of too
many children?*

*Before I knew of this possibility You offer,
I rested content — I thought I had control.
But when a conception occurs, how do I weigh the
options? Ten million sperm in each ejaculation;
400,000 immature ova in the ovaries at birth.
You are too generous!*[4]

*I have over-choice. I cannot say "Yes" to all of
Your conceptions for me. I would be weary, die;
I am only one. I have to trust that You are helping
me not only to conceive, but also to choose what to
let grow.*

*I mourn, mourn, cry at the loss of a potential
being or a possible event. I hurt, suffer to thwart
Your possible gift of birth. All the while some others
long to conceive: ideas, jobs, friends, children.
UNJUST DISTRIBUTION OF GOODS. We are unable
to share what we genuinely would like to. I cannot
give another my conceptions, only my births. They
want their conceptions, not my births.*

*I have no end to this prayer. Such responsibility,
such choice, such power. It would be easier to
pretend You were entirely in control. I could pretend
that all Your eggs are intended to be hatched.*

*Help me to lay my weary body and overworked
mind next to you, to lean on You, to feel You, to
sense Your breath, Your love, Your pat on my back.
Help me to know what to whisper to You in
confession and what to celebrate. May I hear You
call my name tenderly, and know that when You
call, You follow my name with, "My precious child."*

POWER

Prayer is addressed to a "Higher Power" in the various twelve step programs like Alcoholics Anonymous or Overeaters Anonymous. This address makes explicit what is true in all prayer — that power is a crucial concept. There are differing beliefs about how much power the Deity has and how much humans have. Does the power of one usurp the power of the other, cooperate with the other, or persuade the other? If God is "all powerful" it is difficult to understand human responsibility. If God longs for peace and justice, can God make justice happen, regardless of human behaviors, or is God dependent upon humans to do our part? If God is dependent upon us, we need to discern how God convinces and enables us to change.

Some of the time the person who prays longs to have an All-powerful God, for that notion provides a sense of security. It is common to pray to Almighty God, but we need most of the time to envision a cooperative power with the Deity, to think of ourselves as responsible partners in the ongoing creation. "Cooperative Power" is a theologically more accurate metaphor with which to begin prayer. It acknowledges the power of the Deity, but suggests that we are involved in the interaction and are required to use some of our internal power, too. The power of one enhances, builds upon, that of the other. The power of God is shared with humans, and humans share their power with God, who shares it back again. If we cooperate, then God's greatest good is able to be accomplished.

A woman may pray to find her right employment. She seeks to be open to Divine Guidance to find the work where she could be needed and where she could be fulfilled by using her talents. Then she looks for the job. She uses her power not only to search for a job, but also to recognize her strengths, to gain appropriate self-respect and self-knowledge, and to seek guidance from human friends. That action on her behalf empowers God. God is better able to guide her, since she is actively involved in the answering process.

To focus attention in prayer upon power located within both the person and God clearly states that each person has internal power. Psychologist Jean Baker Miller defines power as "the capacity to implement."[5] This understanding of power suggests that a person is able to know what she or he wants, to communicate clearly, and to act upon her or his choices. People who can act from internal power are able to use their authority wisely and compassionately. They are also able to challenge the status quo if they or others have not been granted appropriate power by the society. Miller's definition of power is a secular one which does not name the Deity as part of the process. We can enlarge her definition of internal power to be "the capacity to implement, while one is simultaneously being empowered by the Deity."

Women tend to be ambivalent about the use of our internal power. While we want to express ourselves and to act, we often fear that we are wrong to use power or that our power may be destructive of others.[6] Another fear is that a vital use of our power may involve the giving up of important relationships. This association of the use of power and the loss of affiliations is not made by most men. We need to come to believe that we can maintain significant affiliations while we use our inner capacity to express ourselves and to act.

I find that women are not just ambivalent about their use of internal power when that is expressed with other humans, but also when that is in relation to the Deity. There is often a sense that we should be like Mary, the mother of Jesus, who, we are told, acquiesced to God's will for her. But all that happens is not from God. There is indeed a sense in which we can accept a particular situation because we sense that somehow it is part of God's guidance to do so. But there are many situations which call for transformation, not acquiescence, and religion gets in the way of growth if it is taken as a reinforcement of an oppressive status quo.

Theologian Nelle Morton conveyed the impact that a feminine divine metaphor can have upon a woman's "capacity to implement." She said, "Call on God the Mother or the Goddess. What happens? For women she appears. She says your life is a sacred gift. Pick it up. Receive it. Create it. Be responsible for it."[7] In other words, a female divine image can enable a woman to accept the legitimacy and beneficence of her internal power.[8] It is all right, even good, to have power; we are intended to use that power cooperatively with other beings. We need not apologize for it, simply use it wisely.

As men choose a cooperative power model rather than a "power over" model, they are able to use wisely their "capacity to implement," whether that be as fathers, teachers, or factory workers.

As long as men have to pretend that they live up to certain stereo-types, such as the one that they are to be the powerful figure in all situations, then they are not free to experience respect for themselves or their partners as they are. Their respect is contingent upon how they think they are in the eyes of others.

An illustration will show the connection between self-respect and internal power in association with prayer. A married woman who worked in an office, had several children, did all the domestic functions at home (cooking, cleaning, entertaining), and was involved actively in her church and community, wished that she had more help around the house from her family. She feared the use of her internal power and did not respect herself enough to consider herself as important as the other family members. She was often resentful and depressed. She discovered that it made a large difference whether, as she prayed concerning her dilemma, she perceived that she was pleasing her "Heavenly Father," being challenged by her "Divine Sister," given vitality by the "Spirit of Life and Love," or given empathic understanding by her "Divine Mother." When she shifted from pleasing her Heavenly Father to being challenged by her Divine Sister, she realized that she had to take some responsibility for naming her desires and making some changes. She began to claim her wishes and to implement action toward fulfilling them.

As you reflect upon the inferences regarding power, you might discard a divine metaphor if it connoted a kind of power or authority which did not fit with your theology and your current life situation. "Mother" or "Father" are frequently rejected by individuals as Divine metaphors precisely for these reasons. Individuals who reject these parental metaphors usually have some personal experience with a human mother or father which makes it difficult to relate to a parental divine metaphor for a period of time. Of course these paren-tal metaphors are viable choices for many people precisely because of their personal experience with their own parents.

Power and Authority

Powerful One:

*From whence comes my authority? From
whence comes my power?*

*When I go to a doctor, I seem to lose my power
and authority. With the paper clothes I put on a
paper brain.*

*May I accept Your help at the doctor's office, so
that I will maintain my rightful personal power and
appropriate authority over my own body. I will
know how to ask, what to say.*

*From whence comes my authority? From
whence comes my power?*

*I confess that at work I sometimes act as if I know,
but I am not sure. When I pick up my brief case I seem
to pick up the weight of having to know.*

*May I accept Your help today, so that I maintain
my rightful personal power and appropriate
authority in relation to those with whom I work.
I will know how to be vulnerable and when to say,
"I do not know." I will be so filled with Your power
and authority that I can be genuine and honest.*

*From whence comes my authority?
From whence comes my power?*

*When I talk with my parents and my children, I
tend to feel crunched in the middle, caring for two
generations, each
wanting not to be too dependent. I sometimes pick
up more weight than I ought.*

*May I accept Your guidance so that I live my
life in proper relationship. May I differentiate
between caring and living another's life. My
authority comes from You. My power comes from
You. May I accept it's proper expression, so that
I may feel the freedom You give. Amen.*

Responsible Power

Powerful Friend:

I trust You. You give me power and trust me as I use it. Am I trustworthy? Do I abuse power when I am too aware of the effect I have upon others? Do I enjoy my power too much? Or do I deny my power, pretend that I have none, or very little, when all the while there is a purpose which You gave me and expect me to fulfill?

I seek to be open to Your power and wisdom. Amen.

Wise Use of Power

Cosmic Power:

The anniversary of Hiroshima.
Forgive us, God, for destroying Your creation.
May we use this horrible memory to rededicate ourselves to peace and the wise use of power.
Power — I have begun to hate the word. When I hear it, I feel anxious. I wax sentimental; I want so much for the next generations, each one loved so dearly by the generation above.
Evolution — of the fittest. Please, let us not discover that the daisies that bloom so speedily in nuclear radiation are more fit than us!
I want to hope. Help us to hope. Help us to act for peace and not to act for power's sake alone.
Enable us to make peace. Amen.

Fear of Success

Spirit of Love:

> *I think You long for me to fulfill my call.*
> *Why do I doubt so much?*
> *I resist acting, committing myself.*
> *What if I stick my neck out and succeed?*
> *I don't like attention; I feel awkward.*
> *But how can what You want me to do get done, unless I do it?*
> *Feminist psychology books call it "Fear of Success."*
> *I fear Your not succeeding through me.*
> *I think I may also fear Your succeeding through me.*
> *Spirit of Love, love me into knowing and acting with wisdom, courage, and humility.*
> *Thank you.*

A Woman's Tentative Talk

Goddess:

Embolden us so that we say what we mean. May my sisters and I say what we mean without apology, without taking half of it back by the time we finish our sentences, without looking to others to check how it is being received.

I am pained as I hear her talk: never a complete sentence. May she feel enough self-worth and enough authentic power to know that her thoughts, her actions, and her opinions are valuable, as they are. May she know that she certainly can change her mind, but that it is fine to have a mind. May she have such an opinion of herself that the imagined opinions of others does not preoccupy her. May she feel deep, deep acceptance by You and by her sisters and brothers, so that she can be loved into honesty. May she face her incongruities, her uncertainties, her convictions, and her strengths. May she be a whole person and accept that beauty.

May I be patient, please. May I accept this woman and others as they are, even as I help to love them into the future. May I know how to evoke a trustworthy attitude in sisters and in myself.

Amen! Amen!

A Very Present Goddess

Goddess:

>*I can't imagine You absent.*
>*Off to read the newspaper,*
>*Watching sports,*
>*To bed, to work, "out," gone.*
>
>*You are there.*
>*Always.*
>*Even when You seem to be "in the next room,"*
>*I know You'd come running.*
>*I do not think of You as needing time to*
>*Yourself.*
>
>*I think of You as always available.*
>*No "male prerogative."*
>*You are there.*
>
>*Thank you.*

CHOOSING METAPHORS

You might now look at the list of metaphors provided in chapter three (or think of others which are not on the list) and note any which seem vital. Then you could reflect particularly on the implications for self-respect and cooperative power. You are likely to find a few metaphors which seem exciting, dynamic, possibly "right" for now.

A metaphor like "Tyrant" should be rejected, for it would not foster self-respect, and internal power would not be affirmed. On the other hand, it would be difficult to think of a situation in which the metaphor "Friend" would not be appropriate. But there are many metaphors which require more reflection upon the context in order to assess their value for a particular individual, so let us look at a few situations.

When you are small, very dependent upon human parents, you might be strengthened by a Divine Parent image, for the image fits with so much of childhood reality. But a "Best Friend" metaphor for a four-year-old for whom "best friend" is becoming an alluring idea may foster quite exciting beginnings to the abstract thought about the Divine. The child may be offered a prayer to repeat, "My God-Friend is with me." The child may be encouraged to visualize talking with, hugging, or being held by a symbol for the Deity.

A woman in the peak of her career "outside" or "inside" the home is likely to sense internal power as well as respect with a Divine Colleague or Divine Sister. A man whose mother died when he was still young found the idea of a Divine Mother both exciting and comforting; it stressed an interdependence which he had longed for from his own mother.

Our Co-Worker, Colleague, Friend, Ally, Co-Creator, Co-Author all connote cooperative power between God and us. The co-working interchange between God and humans is clear in the way God is named. If you often feel like clay in the Divine-human relationship, with the Deity as the Potter, it might be wise to reflect upon whether you also feel a lack of interdependence and cooperative power in human relationships. Choosing metaphors which elicit a greater sense of our cooperation with the Deity can also encourage us to work toward greater cooperation in our human relationships, because we see all the participants in life as related to each other.

Members of a workshop on prayer reflected upon their ways of naming the Deity in prayer and pondered the "Potter" image. After a while several of them spoke up with excitement, as they had hit upon a more appropriate divine image — Conductor. They reasoned that the Conductor leads and coordinates the orchestra, but depends upon the orchestra members to use their own talents and to be attentive not only to the conductor but also to each other. The discussion of the use of Conductor as a metaphor for God led into important talk about how they understood God to act in their lives. They found themselves acknowledging their interdependence with the Deity and with each other. When they shifted their attention back to the Potter metaphor, several of them expressed that now the image made them feel limp and too dependent upon God's action, as if they had no internal power of their own.

A woman in this workshop proposed "Blacksmith" as a Divine metaphor. She had great familiarity with the making of horseshoes.

She knew how crucial it was for the horse that the blacksmith care to do his or her work right. She could easily visualize the way in which the metal was bent and shaped to be of use.

One member of a woman's prayer group relayed to the others that the metaphor "Divine Mother" would challenge her in significant ways — ways "Father" never had. Another woman said she thought Divine Mother, for her, would bring only comfort, not enough challenge. A third woman, age 63, had been raised in Christian Science and had used the Father-Mother image early in her life. She had dropped that image for the past few decades, for she had a great deal of conflict with her mother and wanted to maintain a "fierce kind of independence" from her. But within the previous year she had finally become more at ease, more accepting of her mother. She noticed that she had started to use the image, Father-Mother God again in her prayers.

Paul Tillich explains that symbols are born, reach maturity and die.[9] This occurs for the symbols of communities; but it also occurs many times in the life of individuals. We cannot force the birth of meaningful metaphors for the Deity. We ought not cling to them after they have died. We need to explore, provide openings for their births, and permission for their departures. Circumstances change; a metaphor which we had used, but allowed to die, may be resurrected with new life and new meaning.

FOR REFLECTION AND ACTION

1. How do you conceptualize your power in relationship to other people? to God? How do you believe that your power and your responsibility are connected?

2. Listen to yourself pray, attending to the self-respect which is evident. Remembering that self-respect means a healthy regard for our dignity as well as the recognition of our obligations, consider whether any changes in your praying would enhance your self-respect *as you pray.*

3. After experimenting with the use of a variety of metaphors for the Deity in prayer (see the *For Reflection and Action* section at the end of Chapter Three), find three to five metaphors which function well for you. Continue to use these to see how they feel to you and how they affect your prayer.

4. Divide a blank sheet of paper into quarters. In the upper left quadrant draw a symbol of the Deity you held as a child. Draw a symbol of your current image for the Deity in the upper right quadrant. In the bottom left quarter draw metaphors which are being born for you, ways you are beginning to think of the Deity. Looking at the first three quadrants, write down in the fourth any common themes you notice and ways you have expanded your thinking.

NOTES

1. Sallie McFague, *Metaphorical Theology: Models of God in Religious Language* (Philadelphia: Fortress Press, 1982) 177-192.
2. A speech made in a workshop led by Hycel Taylor at the Northern Illinois Conference Annual Pastor's Retreat, September 16-18, 1984, p.4
3. Valerie Saivang, "The Human Situation: A Feminine view," *The Journal of Religion* (April, 1960), republished in Carol P. Christ and Judith Plaskow (eds.) *Womanspirit Rising: A Feminist Reader in Religion* (San Francisco: Harper and Row, 1979) 37.
4. Juanita Williams, *Psychology of Women: Behavior in a Biosocial Context* (New York: W.W. Norton and Co., 1977) 205.
5. Jean Baker Miller, *Toward a New Psychology of Women*, 2nd ed. (Boston: Beacon Press, 1986) 116.
6. Ibid., 120.
7. Nelle Morton, *The Journey is Home* (Boston: Beacon Press, 1985) 143.
8. Carol Christ, "Why Women Need the Goddess," *Laughter of Aphrodite: Reflections on a Journey to the Goddess* (San Francisco: Harper and Row, 1987) 121 and Carol Christ and Judith Plaskow, *Womanspirit Rising: A Feminist Reader in Religion* (San Francisco: Harper and Row, 1979) 278.
9. A discussion of symbols can be found in Paul Tillich's *Dynamics of Faith* (New York: Harper and Row, 1957) 41-54.

 Chapter Five

FIVE LITTLE PIGGIES WENT TO PRAY:

Styles of Prayer (Part One)

This little piggy went to market.
This little piggy stayed home.
This little piggy had roast beef.
This little piggy had none.
This little piggy went wee, wee, wee,
    all the way home.

— *Nursery Rhyme*

Before a family meal one member looks to another and says, "Will you pray the grace?" All know what will occur. That one will talk; the rest will listen. A child first learns to note when prayer is occurring in church because she hears the Deity addressed, then, many words, and finally, "Amen." Prayer for most Protestants is talking. But there are other ways in which people of the Judeo-Christian tradition have communicated with the Deity. St. Ignatius of Loyola is known today for his spiritual direction; much of what he encouraged people to do was to use what I call imagery prayer — visualizing biblical scenes and reflecting on them in order to derive personal merit.[1] The Society of Friends are known for worship which in large measure consists of a form of silent prayer. Those in the Roman Catholic and Greek and Russian Orthodox churches use repeated phrases when they pray the "Hail Mary" and the "Jesus Prayer." Most denominations within Christianity celebrate the Eucharist, which is a ritual action that evokes a sense of communication with the Deity. There are variations on the themes, but prayer within the Christian context is likely to use discourse, imagery, silence, repeated phrases, or a special form of action.[2]

Once while telling the story of the five little piggies to my children, I realized that the nursery rhyme could help a person remember these five styles. The piggy going to market represents action prayer; the piggy staying home uses its imagination. Prayer which uses discourse is definitely the "roast beef" of most Christians' prayer life. The piggy with "none" is being silent, and the one yelling "wee, wee, wee" all the way home is practicing repeated phrases.

PRAYER USING DISCOURSE
THE "ROAST BEEF" OF CHRISTIAN PRAYER

All of the prayers in this book to this point have been prayers of discourse, for they proceed in a conversational manner, following the reasoning of the person speaking. Prayer of discourse can be a few words, "Help me," or it can contain many words. It can be written, as for liturgies, or spontaneous, fresh for the occasion. Discourse prayer typifies most pastoral prayers given in congregational worship as well as most private prayers. The person who prays generally talks by sharing confessions, giving thanks, communicating longings, or empathically mentioning others about whom there is joy or a concern.

Karl Barth was one of the strongest advocates of prayer which uses words in discourse with God. His conviction about prayer as discourse was based upon his understanding of Scripture as saying that in prayer we are to ask of God, period. He wanted Christians to be freed from concerns about what they pray for. We can trust that Jesus, as intercessor, will make right the prayer before God.[3] God hears all prayers and answers them according to God's will for us.

The question of what to ask for in discourse prayer can be dealt with as Barth did: Do not worry about what to ask for, simply ask and trust that the request will be considered by God. We ought to ask as freely as a child who asks their parents for comfort in the middle of the night without worrying about the appropriateness of the request. Under the best of circumstances, whether or not the request is granted, the child is loved and is not ridiculed or judged for having made the request. An advantage of this view of prayer is that it relieves the person who prays from overworrying about whether she or he is praying for the right thing. It enables the person who prays to push through any reluctance to pray by making prayer as trusting and simple as possible. There is great wisdom in Barth's emphasis. Many who worry excessively about what to pray for may be reminded of this position.

A very different view is taken by those in denominations like Christian Science, Unity, and Religious Science. Here the mental thought and the asking processes are taken with enormous serious- ness. You are warned to be very careful for what you pray, for your prayers may be answered just as they are requested. The cleansing is sought before the prayer begins. That is, you are to check to see whether your desires are genuinely the best for others and yourself in the situation. You may even pray to decide for what to pray. For example, a man may want a particular job. If he puts a great deal of energy into his prayers for that particular job, he may very likely get the job. But that may not be God's will, the best for all people who are involved in that situation. Therefore, he would be wiser to be open to the greatest possible good. He may decide to pray "for a fulfilling job in which my talents may be used, and for this particular job to be offered to the right person, considering all of the people involved."

For Barth so much power is in God that we put our trust there entirely. The prayer is "cleansed," answered according to God's will; it is not answered in the sense that the exact request is always granted. A college-bound youth might pray, asking for a car, but she may be accepted to a college in a town with a very good public transportation system, where cars are not necessary. For Christian Scientists or Religious Scientists so much power is in the mental processes which connect humans and the Deity that you must be very clear what you are thinking and saying. Answers may be all-too-closely what you ask for because your mind has such power, since it is connected with the universal mind. These schools of thought might advise the youth to pray for adequate transportation because too close attachment to the request for a car may limit the creative solutions.

Much of the Protestant tradition takes a position between these two poles of divine power and human responsibility. Seldom are Christians told with the boldness of Barth not to take responsibility for checking their asking, to simply trust the power of God. And few Christians take as much responsibility as Religious or Christian Scientists in forming the prayer itself — that seems like too much power and responsibility on the human side of prayer. Most Christian teaching on prayer suggests that we should think beyond our own desires and wishes, to pray in some form for the good of all concerned, but also not to worry excessively about what to pray for.

Self-transcendence — moving beyond your own perspective, to a broader view — should be an important element in the prayer of discourse. Self-transcendence is obvious when we pray for guidance for our national leaders, rather than for our country to get the advantage in political affairs. Transcendence is seen when we pray to be open to understanding and healing in the most creative and viable way, rather than to be specific about what others and we are to do.

Self-transcendence is helpful as we seek to discern answers to prayers of discourse. If you see with a wide view and use many human faculties, such as reasoning, imagination, and feelings, you could discern that accessible public transportation is an enjoyable solution for the young adult as well as being ecologically sound for the city and the planet.

By far the most common grammatical mode used in discursive prayer in the Christian tradition is the imperative mode — one of command or demand. We say, "Make me...," "Keep me...," "Guide them . . ." In formal liturgies we sometimes add, "Lord, hear our prayer." It is as if we are telling the Deity what to do. This type of language puts the burden onto the Deity. Humans ask God and depend upon God entirely to make, to keep, to be with, or to guide. The power is unquestionably with God. Humans are dependent.

An option which is taken far less often in Protestant prayer is the declarative mode found in affirmations. Affirmations make the same "request," but rather than asking the Deity, they affirm in faith that the Deity is doing what we are asking. The emphasis is upon our moving to believe in this divine activity and upon our receptivity to it. In this mode, you would say, "I know that you make me, keep me, are with, or guide them...." Interdependence and the shared cooperative power are more apparent in affirmation prayer because you are aware that you must be receptive to God's guidance. It is not enough that God wants the good; humans must accept and act upon it. Note the wording in the prayer "Power and Authority," page 74. If you affirm, you would say, "I accept Your help at the doctor's office," "I accept Your guidance." If you request, you might say, "Please help me at the doctor's office," "Please guide me." I choose to use the terminology, "May I accept Your help at the doctor's office," and "May I accept Your guidance," because I want both to affirm that the help and the guidance are available and to open myself to be more receptive to God's help.

Some people feel self-respect when they acknowledge their dependence upon the Deity, others feel puny and powerless, dependent in a childish and irresponsible way. They need to acknowledge their role in the answering process in order to ex-perience the respect of self. The first group may find those who emphasize their own role in prayer egoistic or taking too much responsibility in the creative process. But those who place the emphasis upon their role in receiving from God see themselves as taking their share of the interdependent responsibility for creation.

Note the difference in tone and theological beliefs in the following three discourse prayers. The first one is taken from the 1966 *Methodist Hymnal.* It originally appeared in the 1662 *English Book of Common Prayer.* The second was written by Howard Clinebell, professor of pastoral counseling, for a meditation booklet published by the School of Theology at Claremont in 1974. The final prayer can be found in *Guerrillas of Grace,* LuraMedia, 1984; it was written by Ted Loder.

For All Conditions of Men

O God, the creator and preserver of all mankind; we humbly beseech thee for all sorts and conditions of men; that thou wouldst be pleased to make thy ways known unto them, thy saving health unto all nations. More especially, we pray for the holy Church universal, that it may be so guided and governed by thy good Spirit that all who profess and call themselves Christians may be led into the way of truth and hold the faith in unity of spirit, in the bond of peace, and in righteousness of life. Finally, we commend to thy fatherly goodness all those who are in any way afflicted or distressed in mind, body, or estate; that it may please thee to comfort and relieve them according to their several necessities, giving them patience under their suffering, and a happy issue out of all their afflictions. And this we ask for Jesus Christ's sake. Amen.[4]

On Not Wasting My Pain

For my pain O God —
    Which I did not choose
    And do not like,
    And would let go of if I could —
Give me the wisdom to treat it as a bridge
    A crossing to another's pain — to that person's
        private hell.
Grant me the courage not to live alone
    Behind my shell of hiding,
    My make-believe side which tries to always
        seem "on top," in control, adequate for
        any crunch, not really needing others.
Let me own my inner pain so that it will open me
    To those I meet,
    To their pain and caring —
    That in our shared humanity,
    We may know that we are one — in You.[5]

Prayer of Reflection

O God,
    I come to you now
  as a child to my Mother
    out of the cold which numbs
      into the warm who cares.
  Listen to me inside,
    under my words
      where the shivering is,
    in the fears
      which freeze my living,
    in the angers
      which chafe my attending,
    in the doubts
      which chill my hoping,
    in the events
      which shrivel my thanking,
    in the pretenses
      which stiffen my loving.

  Listen to me, Lord,
    as a Mother,
      and hold me warm
        and forgive me.
  Soften my experiences
    into wisdom,
  my pride
    into acceptance,
  my longing
    into trust,
  and soften me
    into love
      and to others
        and to you.[6]

There is a beseeching tone in the first prayer, as if we must convince the Deity to act. The action requested is entirely God's action. If God is pleased, then the results will occur. We are dependent upon the Deity, who has the power. Self-respect is sought through the acknowledgment of dependency upon the Deity.

The second prayer is of a more private nature, but could easily be made into a plural form for a group. This prayer and the third one make requests of the Deity, too, by saying, "Give me the wisdom," "Grant me the courage," "Listen to us inside," "Soften our experiences into wisdom," but the action sought is one of interdependence and cooperative power. I am expected to "own my inner pain," to be "open" to those whom I meet, to gain greater courage to be vulnerable, to accept and to trust. God is not seen as leaving the one who prays alone; God is being asked to help in a cooperative way. The dignity and obligations of the self are most definitely enhanced — increased self-respect is implicit in the prayers.

Because prayer using discourse is the only one of the five styles in which the Deity is virtually always given a name, in the address, there is much potential for identification and affiliation. The "fatherly goodness" of the first prayer and the "Listen to us, Lord, as a Mother," hold potential for those who can identify with fatherly or motherly qualities. They create a sense of "withness," too, for those who can think of themselves as being with a good father or a mother who holds warmly and who forgives.

It is not just that we address the Deity with a name, but also the very fact that we are conversing with an "other" that underscores some of the affiliative benefits of discourse prayer. This is precisely why Paul Tillich did not like prayer of discourse. God, for Tillich, was not an other being with whom to converse. God was Being Itself. According to him, you should not stress the subject-object nature of the relationship, the I-Thouness. You should seek to transcend the two-beings-together aspect of prayer. He knew, however, that humans would continue using discourse prayer. We long for affiliation with the Deity. And talking enhances our sense of that.

Peace on Earth

Peace-Giver:

How blind we are to You! We name missiles "peacekeepers," putting more faith in them than in the peace You try to give us.

How far away You seem at times, especially when we panic and our nations do revengeful acts upon each other, as if You were not present at all.

How much we need You! May we be aware of our need for Your peace instead of the supposed need for harmful weapons. May You be our defense. May we trust in You and use Your gift of creation only to take care of one another.

How close we are to You: nearer than our thoughts of peace; closer than our fear, sadness, and hope; within our very skins; touching our souls; healing our relationships.

Open our eyes, that we may see.
Shalom.

Body Acceptance

Spirit:

You are One who transcends body. Help me to transcend my attachment to my body as a physical being which is to fit into some norm. I am. I am my body, emotions, will, imagination, relationships, spirit, and reason.

As I grieve over the loss of a part of my physical body, I feel Your assurance that I am even bigger in size that counts. I lose, but I gain.

Help me to be aware of my gains, when my losses become dominant in my thinking and feeling. I mourn and feel Your comfort. But I also accept what is to be added to me — strength, love, fullness of being, and the assurance of Your guidance.
Amen.

New Job — New Child — New Roles

Co-Creator:

My stomach is tight. I am aware of being absorbed in myself, rather than the people around me. I am not enjoying my moments right now, but perpetuating resentment and perplexity from the recent past. I know that I am in a state of disharmony. I sense that this is a temporary state, as I readjust my schedule, my thinking, my feelings, to my new life stage. I want to be open to You and Your guidance to see how I can respond to Your highest aims, not only for me, but also for my children and husband.

I am wrestling with intense joy at becoming a mother and longing to do well in my profession. Both jobs are new; I am not sure how well I can do both together. I get short with my husband, and at times I limit my contact with my children. Now when our lives are richer with meaning, more complex, this is a chance par excellence to learn more how to love. Sometimes I feel we are one terrific team: coordinating our possibilities with each other in creative ways. That feels like grace. Why do I not trust those times to dominate? Why do I repeat the times, rehearsing them in my head, when I feel unfairly dumped on?

I trust that we will work out this new stage beautifully, not once and for all, but with a continuing creativity, so that I do not rehearse privately the limiting aspects. I feel my stomach relaxing. I trust You and appreciate my family and my job. Our little world and the large world are both important. I trust Your wisdom in discerning how to balance my responsibilities to each. And I know time changes the emphasis.

Thank you, Challenger.

Counting to Three

God On Whom I Can Count:

> *One, two, three*
> > *...this emergency will subside.*
> *One, two, three*
> > *...this confusion will be resolved.*
> *One, two, three*
> > *...I have all the time I need.*
> *One, two, three*
> > *...God is guiding us here.*

Blood and Water

Creator:

> *You created me with the aid of water. I lived, moved, had my being in my mother's womb, wet. I was born amidst blood, bathed in water, fed milk. I knew how to drink, to wet.*
>
> *Now, today, I allow myself to trust, completely trust, Your continuing creation of me. I trust the blood in my arteries and veins as it cleanses and carries necessary ingredients. I bless the leftover blood of my uterus, no fertilized egg this month. I trust the water in my body as it purifies, gives life to my cells, and takes away impurities.*
>
> *Christ's blood is mixed with water. The sacred and the ordinary join. Communion is ready. Communion is in my body, if I but recognize and accept it. The sacred and the ordinary join in me. I am holy. I trust. I trust. I trust.*
>
> *May I be guided to take gentle care of Your creation, my body temple. May I rightly cherish the juices you lavishly and joyously share.*

IMAGERY PRAYER
THE PIGGY WHO STAYED HOME

Imagery often accompanies discursive prayer, as when you pray for health and also mentally "see" the body as healthy, "feel" optimal functioning, or "hear" the music of the vital organs making joyous harmony. In contemporary practice a number of counselors and medical doctors are using directed imagery to aid their clients' healing processes. Some imagery prayer is quite like intercessory or petitionary prayer in that you visualize things as you believe the Deity is calling them to be. For example, you image a child functioning well in school while consciously thinking of the Deity acting in that child's life as wisdom, harmony, and guidance. But rather than just verbalizing this wish, you visualize the child cooperating in physical education, doing her homework with interest, responding to questions in class, and getting along well with friends. The imagery assists you to sense that the change can take place, and in so doing, it also changes you, the one who prays. The situation is seen in a new way.

One very simple use of imagery in prayer is to visualize a situation or concern surrounded by light. Seeing light around the members of a family which is in the midst of difficulties, visualizing light around a person whom we love, imaging a city in which there has been turmoil as filled with light — all these are ways of becoming aware of the Spiritual Presence in the people and situations. The visualization is both directive and receptive. The person who prays is open to the light, and to a changed attitude about the situation, but also there is energy directed toward the area of concern.

Another way to use imagery in prayer is to attend to symbols and images which arise when we are guided to think of certain scenes. Jesus' parables evoke a rich array of images — mustard seeds, seeds landing on various turfs, hidden treasures, laborers at work, sibling rivalries, shepherds looking for lost sheep, a woman looking for a lost coin. Spiritual disciplines such as St. Ignatius' "Spiritual Exercises" have grown out of reflection upon the rich images of the Bible. Ignatius prepared his exercises in 1533 in order to guide his fellow priests and lay people in devotional work. He suggested that you envision yourself as being present in the dramatic moments of Christ's life, interacting with the people and asking for guidance. An intentional effort is made to receive wisdom regarding your current issues as you explore the meaning of the symbols which are brought forth in imagery.

A decade ago I wrote a book entitled *Opening to God: Guided Imagery Meditations on Scripture*[7] in which I included thirty examples of imagery prayers using biblical themes to initiate the visualization. There are a number of books which help you to follow non-Biblical guided imagery meditations. Often these are based upon Psychosynthesis therapeutic techniques.

GUIDELINES FOR USING IMAGERY

Whether you allow a scene to emerge, follow a guided prayer, or visualize warmth or light around situations and events, it is wise to know some basic guidelines for using imagery and for understanding the images. I suggest seven primary guidelines.

1. Many people think that they are expected to "see" clearly when they "image." But, in fact, most people just "get a sense" of an image. Some people are more attentive to sounds, others to colors or fragrances, and still others to a tactile quality.

2. Imagery improves with practice.

3. It is important to know that whatever occurs in the imagery is all right. You do not need to feel embarrassed or worried about whether you are "doing" it right or succeeding. Simply allow the images to emerge and attend to them.

4. If something happens which appears to be scary or worrisome, you can include assistance in the imagery itself. For example, if you are swimming and get tired, then you can create a life boat, an inner tube, or a helicopter to come to your aid. Wise people or religious symbols can appear to bring comfort or

assistance. Since we are always conscious of what we are doing, we can introduce healthy, helpful images.

5. At times it seems that 'nothing' is happening. Actually, you may be seeing a color, experiencing frustration, daydreaming about other things to do, or you may be resistant to the prayer. All of these are "something," not "nothing," and acknowledging what is taking place may lead to insight or to refocusing upon the prayer itself.

6. Recall that the images are just for the present. It is tempting to hold on to positive images a long time because they were very nourishing. It is also possible to be worried by "negative" images long after their messages were useful. Once I saw a "barren" field when I imaged the plantings of seeds. That was an accurate portrayal of my feelings about my life at that point in time, but that time was very brief. It would not be helpful to continue to think of myself as "barren" because I once, a long time ago, had that image. So it is wise not to get too attached even to meaningful symbols, for they serve their time and we become ripe for other fresh symbols.

7. Just as you can gain more value from nighttime dreams if you record them and work with them, so too, you can gain greater insight from imagery prayer if you write down what happened, tell the images to another, draw pictures, or make the symbols come alive in some way. In some schools of psychotherapy this is called "grounding," since you bring what was not very tangible "down to earth," into your reflection, making connections with daily life.

The following is an example of a guided imagery prayer, based upon images which emerge from reading the Scriptures.

Serving/Being Served

Reading: John 13: 3-15 (RSV)

Jesus, knowing that the Father had given all things into his hands, and that he had come from God and was going to God, rose from supper, laid aside his garments, and girded himself with a towel. Then he poured water into a basin, and began to wash the disciples' feet, and to wipe them with the towel with which he was girded. He came to Simon Peter; and Peter said to him, "Lord, do you wash my feet?" Jesus answered him, "What I am doing you do not know now, but afterward you will understand." Peter said to him, "You shall never wash my feet." Jesus answered him, "If I do not wash you, you have no part in me." Simon Peter said to him, "Lord, not my feet only but also my hands and my head!" Jesus said to him, "He who has bathed does not need to wash, except for his feet, but he is clean all over; and you are clean, but not all of you." For he knew who was to betray him; that was why he said, "You are not all clean."

When he had washed their feet, and taken his garments, and resumed his place, he said to them, "Do you know what I have done to you? You call me Teacher and Lord; and you are right, for so I am. If I then, your Lord and Teacher, have washed your feet, you also ought to wash one another's feet. For I have given you an example, that you also should do as I have done to you."

Biblical Note:

It was a part of eastern hospitality to wash the feet of guests, but that task was usually done by a slave when the guests arrived, not by the master at the dinner itself. (A disciple might occasionally wash the feet of a rabbi.)[8] There are various opinions about the meaning of Jesus' gesture. The action could have been an example of service to one another and the reversal of roles as would be practiced in the Kingdom of God. Or the foot washing might have been a symbolic act in which Jesus reminded the disciples of the service he had done for them, but which they would only later understand.[9] Schnackenburg argues that the washing represented the saving activity of Jesus giving of himself in death.[10]

Peter at first thinks quantitatively, that more washing would be better. But John constructs the story to show that Jesus intended a different kind of meaning to the washing. Jesus is conveying to Peter, "You are clean." Bultmann suggests that this word from Jesus to Peter meant that Peter was already clean, but that Peter would not realize that until the passion and the resurrection.[11]

Guided Imagery Meditation:

Take a few deep breaths, relax, and seek to let go of any lingering thoughts. Become aware of the Presence of God moving through you as you receive images and symbols.

Now get a sense of eating dinner with a gathering of friends. Note where you are and who is there. Notice your feelings about being yourself, about being at the dinner. Note details, like the fragrances, the colors, what is being eaten, who is talking and what they are saying.

Now you realize that the Christ is eating with you. The Christ, being with you and soon leaving, gets out a basin of water and comes over to you, starting to wash your feet. What is your reaction? Allow yourself and the Christ to interact in any way you need to. Take time to allow the interchange to be completed. You may visualize how others are interacting.

The Christ moves away and speaks to all who are gathered, "If I have washed your feet, you also ought to wash one another's feet. For I have given you an example, that you also should do as I have done to you." Take all the time you need to note how you feel, what you think, and what you do.

The Christ must leave. Say good-bye in whatever way you choose, knowing that although you bid farewell now, the Presence of Christ can join you again.

Think back over the events of the supper, the foot-washing, the group being told to wash each other's feet, and the Christ's departure. Then, when you are ready, affirm, "Amen."

Debriefing:

If this imagery prayer is done in a group, it is good for the members to share their images with one another. Whether in a group or alone, it is wise to draw pictures or to make notes of the events which occurred. Include any insights or feelings which come to you in the debriefing process as well as when you were engaged in the imagery prayer. Make connections to any events in your current life. If there is a particular area of spiritual growth which needs attention or focus, you might create a phrase for a prayer of repeated words, as explained later in this chapter.

DISCERNMENT OF MESSAGES
THREE LEVELS OF MEANING IN IMAGERY

Discernment is crucial for both discourse and imagery prayer. How do you know how to interpret events, to know what events are God's answers to the discourse prayers? How do you know how to interpret images, to make sense of them, or to know whether the source was the Deity or your own unconscious mind? We cannot escape the need for discernment, and I am of the opinion that no one style of prayer makes the discernment process any easier. When people are introduced to imagery prayer, it is not unusual for them to balk because they do not know what to do with the images and do not know from whence the images have come — God or self. Yet, days after the discursive prayer, many of us find ourselves seeking to discern whether the events which occur have been God's outpouring or our interference. In both cases, we need much reflection to seek to understand the answers.

Possible meanings of a particular image can be gleaned by analyzing it on three different levels.[12] The first level relates directly to the external world. If I were to receive an image of myself leafletting for a candidate for an upcoming election, I may take that as guidance to act more ardently upon my political concerns in that election. The message may be, "Go, leaflet." In my experience people are often so eager to find the "psychological meanings" of their images that they pass right over the concrete direct message as one option.

A second level upon which to ask, "What does this image tell me?" is one which combines our concrete life situations with a symbolic interpretation. The leaflet image may mean at this level that I should attend to the tree in my yard that needs pruning. The "leaflets" (or little leaves) are coming. Or, on this level, I may be receiving guidance to sublet the apartment to the "Leaf" family. Or I may need to "distribute" my opinions more clearly, or in a different arena than I have been doing. There are myriad possibilities for interpretation at this level. As you work on the interpretation, you can simply let ideas come to mind, jot them down, then see what brings wisdom into your life situation. After using the imagination in the prayer itself, you continue to use your reasoning, intuition, and emotions to discern what guidance may be forthcoming.

The third level is entirely symbolic. This is the level which the Gestalt school of therapy uses virtually all the time when working with dreams or imagery. Here I ask myself what the meaning is if I were all the various parts of the image scene. In other words, in what way am I like a leaflet? What is my message to the world? Who is passing me out, that is, who is advocating my message? What causes do I represent? How boldly am I stating my convictions? Am I being tossed around, unappreciated? Then I ask myself similar questions, as if I were distributing the leaflets. "How do I share? How do I travel, walk, ride, climb?"

I recommend looking at all three levels for each imagery prayer or each image that occurs accompanying other prayer. There may very well be messages at all three levels, some of which do not even relate to each other in a very clear way. Of course, meanings may emerge on only one level. There are times when you get stuck. You have a hard time thinking of any possible message or the messages which suggest themselves simply do not seem to make sense at the moment. It is valuable in this type of prayer to record the images along with their reflections, for it is remarkable how frequently an image makes more sense in a few days or weeks. Rereading at periodic intervals what you have observed in imagery prayer is well-advised.

SPONTANEOUS IMAGERY PRAYER

Rather than initiating a set scene, you can engage in imagery prayer by closing your eyes and allowing any scene to emerge spontaneously. Then you follow the images, seeing in a kind of waking-dream what will occur. Because you are conscious and have control over the visualization, you may direct the images deliberately either to include symbols which tend to evoke wisdom or to introduce symbols which will bring assurance or encouragement.

I summarize here the experience of a young male Roman Catholic seminarian who used imagery which was spontaneous. I did not suggest any of the scenes which he saw in his imagination, though he did relay the images to me verbally as they occurred, and I encouraged him to continue to explore the images. He began by waiting, with his eyes closed, until a scene emerged. Then he saw a lake in his mind's eye and noted many details about the lake. After various observations, he decided to walk along a path. At one point he noted that there were several paths and felt that he must choose one. On this chosen path he had quite a meaningful encounter with a tiny flower. He was drawn to "her" and talked with her tenderly. The little flower spoke with him, giving him advice. Later he noted a few more little flowers. He was very moved, sat down, and talked at length with these flowers. He realized that he was next to a large tree with thick bark. He encountered the bark, talking to it rather boldly and disagreeing with it at times.

In his reflection, he noted that the delicate, what he called, "feminine" side of himself was begging for attention and was a really beautiful side. The "bark" seemed like a particular male, whom he decided he needed to go face. There were many other meanings upon which he pondered, and only he could really grasp the significance of his own imagery.

One of the emotionally satisfying factors of imagery prayer is the immediacy of the response. If we believe that the Deity is a participant in the imagery process, then it is natural to sense interdependent affiliation, based upon cooperative power, shared with the Deity. Because there is so much insight into the self readily available from this form of prayer, I have witnessed hundreds of people blossom with a deepened self-respect when they played with the meaning of their own images. Remember that I mean by self-respect "a healthy regard for our dignity as well as the recognition of our obligations."

An example of personal insight which both affirms and confronts is given by a woman who sought to have an honest appraisal of her relationship with a friend. She asked the Deity to help her to see that relationship from a larger perspective. She visualized that person and herself interacting. Various images appeared. One image was of the friend bowing down to her. She reflected upon whether she was too domineering, or the friend too subservient. She recollected Joseph's dream in the Hebrew Bible which included a similar theme. Another image showed the friend and herself at the end of a limb of a large tree. She laughed a bit as she reflected whether they had "gone out on a limb together."

It is difficult to assess the potential for identification in imagery prayer. Perhaps the identification which occurs is primarily that you participate in the creative process, even as God does. The Deity is often not addressed in imagery prayer, so no particular metaphor needs to be used. This is an asset for group prayer, since each person will have metaphors which are private. If you choose to do so, you could of course name the Deity with a metaphor before entering into the imagery. For example you might say, "Maker of Heaven and Earth, I am receptive to the images you make through me as I see my friend and myself, seeking to discern guidance regarding our relationship." Or you could start, "Source of Light and Peace, I see Light surrounding_____."

The prayers below are imagery prayers based on the concerns of the discourse prayers found in this chapter. Clearly when a prayer of discourse is said in a group it can only convey the particular experience of the speaker, though she or he may try to be attentive to the beliefs and needs of the listeners. When a group enters into imagery prayer, the prayer becomes very personal to each participant. While the group members pray together, the images are unique to the individuals. The group can share after the imagery prayer, seeking to help each other to gain insight from the images which emerged.

Peace on Earth
(Imagery)

Take a few slow, deep breaths and relax. In your imagination, see your community flooded with the Peace of God. Where there has been injustice, see the light of justice. Where there has been poverty and hunger and people without housing, see needs being met. See God's peace and God's justice permeating the community.

Move in your imagination to the community to your east. See that community immersed in the peace and justice of God. Proceed, slowly, around the world, moving from community to community, nation to nation. Where there is upheaval, see answers being found. Where there is bloodshed, see peace treaties being signed and arms being laid down. Where there is misunderstanding, see negotiations going on.

Proceed until you return home. See again your community flooded with the peace of God. If there is any place around the world which comes to your mind as a place of concern, return there in your imagination, and visualize the peace of God there.

Sense your very own body permeated with peace. When you are ready, affirm, Shalom.

Body Acceptance
(Imagery)

When you are relaxed, imagine looking into a mirror. You see your body in detail. Now see a symbol for your body, something which represents your body to you. Note your reaction to the symbol and communicate with it, allowing it to interact with you. If this symbol is encouraging, express your gratitude for it, and affirm, "Amen." If this symbol is something which you do not want, allow a symbol to emerge which is appropriate for what you want your body to be. Communicate and allow that new symbol to share with you. You may want to visualize the Christ or a symbol of God's Presence to be with you as you interact with your body symbols. Give thanks for the wisdom gained, and affirm, "Amen."

(It would be good to draw a picture of the symbol or symbols. Looking at the pictures can encourage you to become like the qualities of the positive symbols.)

REPEATED WORDS AS PRAYER
"WEE, WEE, WEE" ALL THE WAY HOME

The repeating of words or phrases emerged as a devotional exercise in both Eastern and Western religions because it is a good way to concentrate (easier than silence for many). Also, it has the virtue of being something you can know you do properly; there is far less ambiguity than in other styles of prayer. Imagery and discourse prayer allow you much creativity and choice, but as you repeat certain words, you do not need to question, or even to think — simply to concentrate. Almost everyone experiences times when she or he can benefit from the simplicity and directness of repeating words.

Some people point out that Jesus told us not to pray with vain repetition (Matthew 6:7). That advice was given in a unique situation, in which the people believed that the Deity would hear them better (or perhaps they would seem more pious to others) if they prayed longer. That is not the reason for repeating phrases in this style of prayer. Here it is the recognition that with repetition one's own self is affected in deep ways. If I repeat, "Love and peace are unfolding" again and again, I accept that affirmation of faith at deeper and deeper levels of my soul and psyche.

In the Christian tradition probably the most used prayer of repetitious words is the Rosary of the Roman Catholic church. As you pray, you hold a chain composed of different-sized beads. With each repetition, the next bead on the chain is held. This eliminates the need to count while praying. You become familiar with what to say at each bead on the chain, so your energy can be put into con-centration upon the words.

Another prayer which uses repetitious words is the "Jesus Prayer." The words to this prayer are quite short and simple: "Lord Jesus Christ, Son of God, have mercy upon me." Since the sixth century this prayer has been used in its present form. It originated at the monastery of St. Catherine on Mt. Sinai and was carried by Gregory of Sinai in the fourteenth century to Mt. Athos in Macedonia. The Greek Orthodox church was the sole user of this prayer until 1782, when the people of Mt. Athos compiled a collec-tion of writings which consisted of their experiences with the prayer. About ten years later this book, entitled *Philokalia* ("Love of the Beautiful"), was translated into Russian. In this form it was intro-duced into the Russian Orthodox church, where it was widely used.[13]

Unlike the Rosary and other types of repetitious prayer, the Jesus Prayer is not done at given times with total concentration solely upon that. It is prayed while in the midst of other activity, as a prayer which is constantly on the lips, again and again. After a while the prayer moves from being just upon the lips to being a "prayer of the heart."[14]

Many people to whom I have introduced this prayer have found it meaningful. Some made alterations to suit their situations and needs. One person repeated the phrase again and again, as it was, then began to alter it to make it into a form of intercession. She said, "Have mercy upon her, him..." thinking of a particular person.[15] A young woman wrote in her prayer journal:

As I began, I drew some comfort that this prayer . . .
has been, like Jesus, like me, a part of salvation history. I
knew what it meant for God to have mercy on Sarah, on
Ruth, on Esther, and all of the mothers of my faith. Then I
knew what it was like for Jesus to have mercy on the
woman at the well, on Mary and Martha, on his mother. I
knew then that Jesus had mercy on Corazon Aquino, on
my sister, on me, "Lord, Jesus Christ, Son of God, Have
mercy on us."[16]

Protestant churches have not used repetitious words as a style
of prayer nearly as much as the Orthodox and Roman Catholic traditions. The Lord's Prayer is recited in many churches once a week,
but simply reciting a prayer every week does not enable you to
understand the effects of repetition. One Protestant group which
uses a creative form of repetitious prayer call themselves the Fellowship of Contemplative Prayer. They recite daily one "I Am" statement of Jesus. They say, for instance, "I am the Vine," or "I am the
Door." They repeat the same phrase for three months, then change
to recite a different "I am" statement for another three months, rotat-
ing through all the statements, then returning to the first. The
primary word in the statement ("shepherd," or "light" for example),
becomes a "catch" word, upon which they reflect during the day in a
similar manner to which the Jesus Prayer is practiced.[17]

The purpose for repeating a word or phrase may vary. It can be
practiced to increase your concentration and health[18] or to increase
your receptiveness to God and to qualities which you sense God is
guiding you to develop.

The "I Am" statements, the Jesus Prayer, and the Rosary are
prepared texts or phrases to recite. There is yet another alternative,
one that is particularly good if you want to be more in tune with your
own intuitive processes. That alternative is a "life mantra" or
"currently meaningful phrase" obtained by attending to your
dreams, thinking about your strengths and areas of needed growth,
or reflecting with a friend or counselor, to find some particular
phrase which seems appropriate.[19] When I was in a particularly
impatient period in my life I chose: "Wise Patience, Be What You
Are." Another time, when I was feeling vulnerable about my own

creativity, I recited, "Infinite Creator, Be."

Often I ask groups to choose a phrase which they think they could benefit from repeating together. We start out with some ideas, list the ideas, then modify, add, and revise, until some phrase seems right for us. For example, one class which was studying prayer developed the phrase, "God's Spirit: Fill Us with Prayer." After repeating the prayer as a group, they discussed their various experiences with the phrase. They decided to transform the imperative "Fill" to the declarative "Fills." Phrases are changed to make it easier to repeat or because there is a theological point which needs clarification.

One woman said that she frequently awoke with a song on her mind or lips. She took that song or phrase as a "spiritual barometer" on which she reflected. Many black spirituals were and are sung over and over to repeat the hope and faith which the music conveys.

The Gregorian Chant is the sung prayer of the Roman Catholic Church. Its name derives from St. Gregory the Great (d. 604), but the liturgical music tradition began very early in the Christian Church. All the major religions of the world have developed traditions of chant-ing, for it is a common psychological phenomenon that the combin-ing of words, melody, and rhythm in repetition creates beauty and intensity of focus.

Because the amount of repetition and the investment in a phrase is very great, it is important to ask what effect a particular phrase seems to have upon you. You ought never to choose a phrase which is stated in the negative form, such as "Lead me out of temptation." Rather, you should state what you do want; in this case, "God leads me toward the good."

A small sentence in a discourse prayer is surrounded by a con-text which allows for the understanding of the negative, but one sentence alone, repeated so many times, loses its context. In the Lord's Prayer, we do say, "lead us not into temptation," but that is nestled within a prayer which affirms the presence, holiness, and reign of God coming on earth. God is affirmed as daily bread. Much more than the phrase regarding temptation is called to the mind of the person who prays. If all thoughts about God's glory and power were missing, so that we were to repeat only the temptation phrase, we might begin to focus solely upon our own frailties, forgetting

God's creative power in our lives. Because there is so much concentration when a phrase is repeated, and because we are not to
wander off to include other thoughts, exactly what we repeat is
important. It must be something which will benefit from intense
focus — that is, something positive, not something to avoid.

A minister explained to me that when he wishes to pray for
others, but wants to leave open what to pray for on their behalf,
he combines imagery with repeated words. He says the name of
the person over and over while visualizing the person in differing
situations or settings. He repeats the name until he "knows"
when to stop, then he moves on to the next individual for whom he
wishes to pray.[20]

The prayer of repeated words undergirds a belief in the revelation of the Deity through the will. In repeating a phrase over and over
again, the will is enlisted and strengthened. As you speak or form the
phrase, you do not allow yourself to daydream; you must come back
to just that phrase. You will yourself to enter into a very receptive
state. For this reason, repeated words as prayer are helpful to use
after a larger prayer of discourse, to strengthen your will and openness with regard to the concern.

The fulfillment of the "twin needs" when you use repeated
phrases is related to the words which are chosen. When I repeated,
"Infinite Patience, be what you are," I was seeking to identify with the
quality of patience. Those who repeat the "I Am" statements of the
Christ are intentionally strengthening their identification with the
qualities which they name. "Thou art my Guide," emphasizes the
desire for interdependent affiliation. Phrases can be used which
underscore strong dependency upon the Deity. This is the tone of
both the Rosary and the Jesus Prayer. "I and the Father are One," or
"I and my Mother are One," would link both the affiliative and
identification needs in one statement which alludes both to
communion and union.

The prayers of discourse and imagery which we have looked at
in this chapter can be summarized in various brief phrases and
repeated either again and again for five to twenty minutes or occasionally and spontaneously throughout the day. You could develop
these phrases after praying in a different style, or you could think of
these phrases as you focused in on the prayer need, intending only

to pray with the repeated words.

"Blood and Water" and "Body Acceptance" are prayers which relate to bodily concerns. It is very helpful to a person in a hospital or one with a physical concern to have a short affirmation which can be repeated whenever doubt arises. "New Job — New Child — New Roles" and "Counting to Three" are prayers given in a time of crisis. At crisis periods, too, short phrases are helpful to remember. I carried around the phrase, "I have all the time I need" in my purse for several years, reminding me that I need not panic, but could befriend time.

Peace on Earth
(Repeated Words)

1. *Peace, peace, peace.*
2. *The Peace of God passes all understanding.*
3. *Peace and justice for all.*

Body Acceptance
(Repeated Words)

1. *Your Presence assures me.*

New Job — New Child — New Roles
(Repeated Words)

1. *I trust Your wisdom.*
2. *Balance unfolds.*

Counting to Three
(Repeated Words)

1. *I have all the time I need.*
2. *God is guiding us here.*

Blood and Water
(Repeated Words)

1. I trust.
2. I take gentle care of Your creation.
3. My body is a temple.

FOR REFLECTION AND ACTION

1. Gather some written prayers of discourse and read them several times. Notice which ones feel like prayers you can pray authentically to God and which do not fit with your experience or your belief about God. Talk to a friend about her or his experience with those same prayers.

2. Practice the imagery prayer based on John 13:3-15, found on page 99, or one of the other prayers in *Opening to God* (Carolyn Stahl, Nashville: The Upper Room, 1977) or another imagery prayer resource. A few days later try the same imagery prayer again. Look back to your first experience, reflecting upon the messages and the changes during the interim.

3. Practice visualizing Light surrounding people, places, or events about which you have love or concern.

4. Choose one of the options for the use of repeated words as prayer: the "Jesus Prayer," the Rosary, the "I Am" statements of Jesus the Christ, or a personal "life mantra." Practice repeating the phrase fifteen minutes once or twice a day for several days, then reevaluate whether you need to change the phrase in any way. Continue to practice for several months.

NOTES

1. St. Ignatius, *The Spiritual Exercises* (New York: Image Books, 1964) 54-104.
2. These categories are not entirely discrete; some particular prayers may fit into more than one category. There are, no doubt, events which some Christians call prayer which do not fit into any of these categories.
3. Karl Barth, *Church Dogmatics* (Edinburgh: Clark, 1961) III/4,94.
4. *The Methodist Hymnal* (Nashville: The Methodist Publishing House, 1966) #742.
5. Howard J. Clinebell, Jr., *Meditations for Churchmen in the Seventies*, 3d ed., by the faculty and Administration of the School of Theology at Claremont, 1974, 16.
6. Ted Loder, in *Guerrillas of Grace: Prayers for the Battle* (San Diego: LuraMedia, 1984) 16.
7. Carolyn Stahl, *Opening to God: Guided Imagery Meditations on Scripture* (Nashville: The Upper Room, 1977).
8. Barnabas Lindars, *The New Century Bible Commentary: The Gospel of John* (Grand Rapids: Wm. B. Eerdmans Publ. Co., 1972) 441-456.
9. Lindars emphasizes the discipleship theme; Bultmann shows the paradox of the two themes held together. Rudolf Bultmann, *The Gospel of John: A Commentary* (Philadelphia: Westminster Press, 1971) trans. G R Beasley-Murray, et. al., 457-474.
10. Rudolf Schnackenburg, *The Gospel According to St. John*, Vol. III (New York: Crossroad, 1982), trans. David Smith and G. A. Kon. Original edition: 'Das Johannesevangelium,' III Teil. (Verlag Herder. Frieburg Im Breisgau, 1975) 15-26.
11. Bultmann, loc. cit.
12. Ann Faraday, *The Dream Game* (New York: Harper & Row, 1974) 138-141.
13. Per-Olof Sjogren, *The Jesus Prayer* (Philadelphia: Fortress Press, 1975) 11-16.
14. Sjogren, 28-36.
15. Kathy Robothom, in "Christian Prayer: Expanded Options" class at United Theological Seminary, Spring, 1986.
16. Cynthia D. Alte, in the same class.
17. Comments made by Brion Endicott of the Fellowship of Contemplative Prayer, Bakersfield, CA, August 26, 1975.
18. Harold Bloomfield, et. al., *TM: Discovering Inner Energy and Overcoming Stress,* (New York: Delacorte Press, 1975) 91-114.
19. The concept of "life" and "text" mantras comes from a seminar led by John Biersdorf, of the Institute for Advanced Pastoral Studies, September 23-26, 1975.
20. The Reverend Preston Price, San Diego, CA.

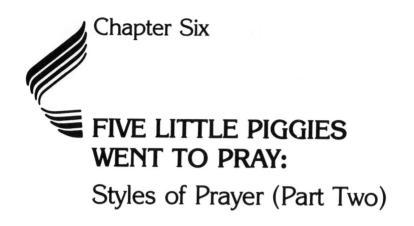

Chapter Six

FIVE LITTLE PIGGIES WENT TO PRAY:

Styles of Prayer (Part Two)

Finite but with Infinite Capacities

Infinite One:

May we have a right perspective on our very real finitude as well as our infinite capacities.

May not fool ourselves into thinking that we can live forever or that we are capable of doing or being all things, even for a few people. May we not be self-sufficient. Yet may we not put limits on our capacities. May we never limit what You can do through us. May we have a little more wisdom, a little more love.

We hope for and expect much. May we know when these hopes are too high or too low. May You accelerate us or put on our brakes, in a gentle way.

Gratefully, amen.

SILENCE AS PRAYER
THE PIGGY WHO HAD NONE

God speaks to us most vividly through our imagination in imagery prayer and in our reasoning and emotions as we discern how to understand the symbols produced by that prayer. God can use especially the avenue of human will when we repeat a phrase again and again. When we pray with discourse, we discern God's guidance through reasoning, checking our emotions, and observing events. It is often the experience of the person who prays in silence that God speaks through intuition. We may never "know" in a rational or emotional way what has occurred when we are silent, but often there is a sense that something meaningful has occurred. That "something" need never be "known," even in the future, to have its value.

Silence is much more than the absence of sound. It is not prayer that employs words and sentences on a subvocal level. That is really prayer of discourse, said privately. In silence no words are said or thought. Eastern religions have developed the practice of silence much more thoroughly than Western religions, which are more word-oriented. However, for centuries there have been Christians who have seen the value of silence, both on an individual and group scale. The earliest records of the use of silence were often in connection with solitary prayer. Early in Christian history silent worship became compulsory for many monastic communities, but it did not exist in public worship.[1]

There are three very different types of silence. One is "Waiting Silence," practiced by the Society of Friends (Quakers). It is primarily a group phenomenon, but it can be practiced by an individual, too. The second type of silence is suggested by St. Teresa of Avila, when she speaks of the "Prayer of the Quiet" in the *Interior Castle,* written in 1577. The third type of silence I label "disciplined silence," for it requires strict concentration.

WAITING SILENCE OF THE FRIENDS

Attempts to hold worship with silence as a large ingredient were at first met with great resistance. A society in Paris in 1209 which cultivated silence in order to discover the Inner Presence was broken up as heretical. There were some movements in the fourteenth and fifteenth centuries which allowed silence in worship when it arose. However the first meetings in which silence was not accidental were held by the "Family of Love" in the mid-sixteenth century. The Seekers (small groups in various parts of England) were the first to use what is most like the Quaker silence known today.[2] They were not as silent as the Familists, but in William Penn's words they "waited together in silence, and as anything arose in one of their minds that they thought favored with a Divine spring, so they sometimes spoke."[3] Seekers joined the Quakers very early in Quaker history. The Quakers sought to preserve silence as the prevailing norm, but they wanted to maintain the liberty to speak if one of the members felt drawn to do so. Charles Lamb described early Quaker meetings: "More frequently the meeting is broken up without a word having been spoken. But the mind has been fed. You go away with a sermon not made with hands. You have bathed in stillness."[4]

Today groups of Friends, known to many as Quakers, gather to sit in silence. If a member has a strong urge to speak and senses that the urge is Divine guidance, then she or he does speak. Sometimes the analogy to a well is made: The deep springs within oneself are touched, and the nourishment must be shared. At times the words spoken by various members are connected by theme, but it is possible that there is no logical connection. The Deity's messages are considered to be offered in the Silence as well as in any words which are spoken.[5]

"Waiting Silence" is not easy. The literature of the Friends shows concern over too much speaking which seems not quite inspired, "little more than a political forum," and concern over becoming drowsy or sleepy rather than being attentive and alert to the Inner Presence.[6]

A modified version of the waiting silence could be practiced by an individual alone. You could sit in silence, seeking not to dwell on the myriad items that wander through the mind. But if something arises which you sense to be from that inner well, then you can dwell on that and perhaps even write down some notes for reflection later, then move back into the silence once again.

Notice that in the language which is used to describe this style of prayer there is attention to both the identification and affiliative aspects of prayer. The deep springs within yourself are touched. In silence you cultivate the discovery of the Inner Presence. In other words, as you sit in silence, you feel within your own depths a sense of the Spiritual Presence which is also beyond. But the identification is very close to communion, the deep sharing of yourself with an "other." There is "mutual and reciprocal correspondence with God."[7] The attitude of waiting is an affirmation that there is indeed a transcendent dimension of the Deity upon which to wait. You wait to be quiet, to allow the "Other" which moves through you to make Itself known. As it is known, the spiritual need for "withness," affiliation with the Deity, is likely to be met.

PRAYER OF THE QUIET
ST. TERESA OF AVILA

Seven mansions are described in what St. Teresa of Avila called the "Interior Castle" of prayer. The Prayer of the Quiet occurs about midway through the journey, after you are well-established in prayer and meditation. Rather than trying to achieve silence, this quiet comes upon you as a gift of God. It is a kind of hush which may occur regardless of what you are doing. St. Teresa called it "the greatest peace and quietness and sweetness within ourselves."[8]

St. Teresa used a water metaphor to explain the difference between this unsought quiet and the fruits which accompany the worked-for meditation. Two large basins are filled with water in different ways: In one the water comes from a long distance, with the aid of human skill, but "the other has been constructed at the very source of the water." The water brought by human skill corresponds to the spiritual sweetness produced by meditation or prayer which is worked for. "It reaches us by way of the thoughts; we meditate upon created things and fatigue the understanding; and when at last, by means of our own efforts, it comes, the satisfaction which it brings to the soul fills the basin, but in doing so makes a noise." But the Prayer of the Quiet "fills without making any noise."[9]

This type of silence is conscious communication as it takes place, for you are aware of the encounter and nonverbal communication with the Deity, but you do not initiate this type of prayer.

DISCIPLINED SILENCE

Disciplined silence has been used for centuries by Zen Buddhists, who call quiet sitting *zazen*.[10] As in waiting silence, there is an attempt to concentrate, but unlike waiting silence, disciplined silence does not "wait" for any words to come. There is an expectation to maintain the silence, to go deeper and deeper into it, as your distracting, fleeting thoughts become less frequent. You seek to let go of any thought, body sensation, or feeling. When something comes to your attention, it is simply recognized, then released. This silence is difficult to practice, for as soon as you seek not to think, you discover all the thoughts and sensations which persist as chatter in the mind. You need not be apologetic or feel guilty about these distractions. Simply recognize their presence and dismiss them for the time being. Of course if you do feel guilty or apologetic, then you acknowledge those feelings and thoughts and seek to let go even of those.

The Deity is not addressed in this form of silence. No "request" is made. No dialogue occurs. Yet I experience silence not infrequently as confessional. As I sit, seeking to let go of any thought, sensation, or feeling, I become aware of my fleeting thoughts which repeat with absurdity. The pettiness and repetitiousness of those thoughts remind me of how I limit the Spiritual Presence by my preoccupations. More than "thinking" about what to "confess," as I might in the prayer of discourse, I find myself face to face with myself, and that confronts me with how I choose to live and what I could do instead. A woman in a prayer group commented that she found this type of silent prayer to be compatible with one of the ethical challenges of Christianity: to transcend one's preoccupation with one's own thoughts once in a while!

Zen Buddhists do not think of an "other" with whom you pray. Yet, I am convinced that if you enter into disciplined silence with a prior expectation that sharing with the Deity is taking place, then at an unconscious level, that communication occurs. Some Christians practice this silence before using other types of prayer. It helps you to become centered, relaxed, and open. Some argue that this is a "spiritual discipline," not prayer, because the communication which takes place is not conscious. However, the *decision* to enter into the time of attention *is* conscious. Therefore, you are consciously opening yourself to communication with the Presence of God, knowing that much of that communication will be at an unconscious level.

For many in our busy, vocal society, silence is not appreciated at first. One member of a prayer group found that she simply could not practice the disciplined or waiting form of silence, the first few times we tried them as a group. She kept feeling she ought to be "doing something" with her time. So she chose to use discursive prayer, subvocally. The group continued to practice the five styles of prayer, including these forms of silence, and within a month she, more than any other member of the prayer group, appreciated the freedom which silence brought. Silent prayer began to enable her to release her concerns for a while. She discovered as she practiced it, that silence was a time of handing over the concerns, of shelving them, while she focused attention solely upon the Presence of Spirit.

With silence as a group experience there is a large sense of interdependence and of shared cooperative power. Even those who do not speak in "waiting silence" are affirmed as participating fully, for the intention is to be silent. This is quite different from the experience of a group which is practicing discourse prayer, for those who remain quiet are generally perceived as "not praying." More than in any of the other four prayer styles, silence does not depend upon a "leader." All share together in common.

ACTION PRAYER
THIS LITTLE PIGGY GOES TO MARKET

I have associated action prayer with the little piggy going to market because that was the most active piggy. But this "Going to Market" image is especially appropriate when you reflect upon the Zen ox herding pictures, which present the faith journey of a holy man who is practicing Zen Buddhism. In the final stage, after much prayer and isolation from others, he returns to the marketplace. He knows who he is, as one with the Buddha nature, so he is no longer searching; rather, wherever he goes, life blooms.

> With bare chest and feet he enters the market.
> His face is smeared with earth, his beard covered
>   with ashes.
> A huge laugh streams over his cheeks.
> Without humbling himself to perform miracles or
>   wonders, he suddenly makes the withered
>   trees bloom.[11]

There are some people who have so dedicated themselves to prayer that their acts tend to become prayer. They have united their activity with their communication with the Deity. But most action, no matter how dedicated or loving, is not actually prayer, for most of the time action is not consciously connected with communicating with the Deity. Prayer can of course motivate you to act, but acts are seldom in themselves, "conscious communication with the Deity." There are at least two different forms of action which qualify as prayer: "Practicing the Presence" and what I will call "meditative and ritual action."

PRACTICING THE PRESENCE

Brother Lawrence was a lay brother among the barefooted Carmelites in Paris in the latter half of the seventeenth century. He is well known as one who was assigned to the kitchen to work but who developed an action-oriented way to engage in prayer in the midst of his tasks. (It is important to understand that kitchen work was considered "naturally a great aversion.") He came to believe that "our sanctification did not depend upon changing our works, but in doing that for God's sake which we commonly do for our own."[12] His method of prayer was to think of God frequently while engaged in all of his tasks. It is "a great delusion to think that the times of prayer ought to differ from other times."[13] He argued that we must know before we can love, and in order to know God, we must think of God often. Speaking of God, Brother Lawrence said, "When we come to love Him, we shall also think of Him often, for our heart will be with our treasure."[14]

Thinking of the Deity while we are engaged in our activities could be like having many discourse prayers throughout the day, but Practicing the Presence need not have a conversational tone; it is rather a frequent reminder of God, just thinking, "God," while you act.

Especially women and manual laborers may find it offensive to receive the advice "think of God while doing tasks you do not like." This method can be used to make us accept unchosen or stereotypic roles complacently. But that misuse of this style of prayer does not negate the potential it has for truly enlivening some of our activities — both those which we have a natural inclination to enjoy and those which we dislike.

All of us can find our own activities which are conducive to the Practicing of the Presence. Waiting is a good time to practice. When we wait for a traffic signal, wait for a lecturer to finish, wait for our date to arrive, wait for our teenagers to return home, or wait for a ride, we can experience God's presence. While nursing a baby in the middle of the night, mowing or weeding the lawn, shoveling snow, sunbathing, swimming, riding a bus, we can Practice the Presence. It is probably easier for most people who seriously want to practice this form of prayer to choose a particular event during which they will practice regularly, for the event itself becomes a reminder to practice.

MEDITATIVE AND RITUAL ACTION AS PRAYER

Meditation refers to techniques for spiritual or personal growth which may be used with or without attention to the Deity. You may "meditate" upon a rose in order to develop some of the qualities which that rose symbol evokes, qualities of wholeness and maturity. Or you may focus upon a cross, a star, or a candle flame, seeking to let go of thoughts other than those which relate to that symbol. (This is similar to repeating a phrase, but uses the visual sense rather than the vocal and auditory one.) Just as it is possible to repeat phrases in order to develop concentration or health, these visual practices can be done for personal enrichment without any thought of or even belief in the Deity. But if you enter into these activities seeking to be receptive to the Spiritual Presence then the visual practices certainly are prayer. Focusing upon symbols especially strengthens your ability to identify with some aspect of the Deity.

Rituals are certainly diverse. The morning ritual of showering, brushing teeth, reading a newspaper, and eating breakfast may be quite precise, well-timed, and reenacted daily. In contrast, the ritual of baptism may occur in worship only a few times a year in a given congregation. Rituals can simply be repeated activities, but when they are combined with attention to communication with Divinity, they are prayer. Perhaps the most profound example for many Christians is the ritual of the Eucharist where you take bread and wine attentive to communication with the Divine Presence.

In order to meditate, your attention must be focused. The focus can be visual, aural, mental, or one of repeated activity. For this reason, forms of meditation can vary widely. We can concentrate on our breathing or upon a mental thought or paradox. (In one school of the Zen Buddhist tradition paradoxes called *koans* are the focus of the meditator's attention.) We can sing hymns, play an instrument, or listen to music with such exclusive focus that it becomes a meditative or ritual action. Ritualistic dance combines a variety of foci for concentration — music, repetitive movements, and visual cues.

Dancing and whirling were some of the very oldest religious acts. In the mystical tradition of Islam this ritual dancing and whirling was developed to a fine art in the sixteenth and seventeenth centuries by those in the Mideastern Islamic Mevlevis convents, who became known as the Whirling Dervishes.

Whole congregations of Christians engage in body gestures such as lifting arms, standing to sing, kneeling to pray, or walking to receive communion. Their very movement tends to focus attention upon God's presence. Liturgical dance usually involves a few people who give movement to prayer, poetry, or music. Although the ritual action is done only by the dancers in most cases, their meditative action often helps the observers to focus attention on the transcendent dimension in the midst of worship.

Practicing the Presence and meditative or ritual action as prayer are diverse activities. They have in common the fact that communication with the Deity takes place while we are engaged in activity. In both, we intend to pray and are consciously engaging in the prayer activity.

In Chapter One I defined prayer as "conscious communication with the Deity." I believe that we are communicating with the Deity at all times, even when we are not conscious of the communication taking place, but I do not call that unconscious process prayer. There are times when we take action in which, either in the moment of activity, or upon later reflection, we feel that we are or were very attuned to God. We may be taking action to bring about greater justice or healing in a situation. We may be visiting a friend in the hospital or participating in a twelve step program. Or, we may feel attuned to God as we talk with a friend, finding just the right words to say or the right time to be silent. I am not calling these times prayer because we are not consciously communicating with the Deity at the moment.

These moments of action surely can be part of the process of answers to prayer, or there may be moments of prayer in the midst of these activities. For example, if I am talking with a friend, and I think, "Heavenly Friend, help me to know what to say," then a little later, "Thank You, for Your guidance," I have had two tiny prayers in the midst of the conversation with my friend. I may not even ask for help, but experience help which seems transcendent, like grace. If I have an awareness of this grace, then that thought becomes a prayer acknowledging God's communication to me.

I believe that we may often follow God's guidance without being aware of that guidance, just as we may do that which God is guiding us not to do, without being aware of that. Neither of these unconscious phenomena I label prayer. Recall that I do not believe that prayer is particularly more holy than other acts. There are people who very rarely consciously communicate with the Deity. According to my definition of prayer, they rarely pray. However, they may regularly act upon God's guidance, without conscious attention to that fact or experience.

USING ALL FIVE PRAYER STYLES
EACH PIGGY IS NEEDED

Just as some people gain greatest insight into knowledge when they read the printed word, other people learn when they hear a lecture, and still others when they get to practice what is being taught. Likewise, people vary in the avenues through which they best receive Divine guidance. Students of knowledge wisely use as many modes as possible to foster learning; those who pray wisely include many avenues for receiving guidance. These five styles of prayer lead to receptivity through the will, imagination, intuition, reasoning, emotions, aesthetic sensitivities, and the body. A combination of these styles enhances the enjoyment and effectiveness of prayer for individuals and for groups.

While these styles are usually practiced independently of one another, it is helpful at times to combine the styles while you pray. I have put them together into "mini-marathon" prayers when I have introduced these five styles to groups. These sessions usually require about an hour; however, if there is a short amount of time or the intent is simply to demonstrate the styles, they can be done more rapidly. A group or individual could take several hours to pursue these sessions more conscientiously. Two such prayer sessions are suggested below.

MINI-MARATHON SESSION ONE

1. Start with disciplined silence for at least five or ten minutes.

2. Allow a symbol to emerge and dialogue with the symbol, then bid it farewell and draw the symbol on paper which has been made available in advance. (These can become nametags.)

3. Move around the room, greeting each other SILENTLY, trying to combine the thought of the Deity with every thought or observation you have; that is, Practice the Presence of God as the greetings occur.

4. Sit down with a globe (or pillow of the world) in the center of the room. One person goes to the world, picks it up, and points to a place on it, offering an intercessory prayer regarding that location. Then another person picks up the world and does likewise. Or pass the world around in a circle, each person praying as they receive the world. (Pillows of the world are great for this, for they can even be hugged.)

5. Out of the group experience thus far, allow a phrase to emerge which is meaningful for the group as a whole. Take some time to make the choice, changing the phrase until there is a consensus that the wording seems right for now. Then repeat the phrase slowly quite a number of times and allow the group to end on its own accord.

MINI-MARATHON SESSION TWO

1. Start with people sharing discourse prayer, however they choose to do that.

2. Share in a guided imagery prayer on images evoked from the Scriptures, such as the one based on the parable of the yeast leavening the bread, found in Luke 13:20-21 or Matthew 13:33. Debrief this amply, by drawing, sharing verbally in small groups, or writing responses.

3. Pass around a loaf of bread and juice. Then, in silence, each person eats the bread and drinks the juice thinking of the Deity ("Practicing the Presence") as much as they can while eating. Try to stay focused, thinking about some aspect of the Deity; gently move your thoughts back, if they wander.

4. Choose a phrase as a group to repeat together. It may relate to the theme of leaven, or bread and juice, or it may be on a theme which has emerged in the sharing. Repeat it for a while, until the group stops on its own accord.

5. Close with waiting silence.

THE JOURNEY AHEAD

We reach a point when we know that we must accept the invitation to pray authentically, to encounter the Deity in ways which are genuine for us. There are many choices which we are required to make. Do we pray in silence, repeat words, talk in prayer of discourse, use imagery, or follow an action style of prayer? How do we think of and name the Deity with whom we pray? Our search is like a journey. The traveling is not always easy, and it takes patience and time. Jesus the Christ, on his journey, was disappointed and impatient with the people of Jerusalem, who had so often not grasped what prophets had told them and were not grasping his message, either. He was sad for them, but shared tenderly with them an image he had, of himself gathering them together, just as a hen gathers her own brood under her wings (Matthew 23:37, Luke 13:34). Occasionally on our way we need to remind ourselves that we are cared for tenderly. We may imagine ourselves enfolded in the protective embrace of our Mother Hen. We are with Her, and in some ways like her. We are able to care for others, even as we let ourselves be cared for.

As tiring and wearisome as the task may be, the journey brings with it numerous times of joy, peace, understanding, and laughter. Our search will be vigorous at times, when our longing is great. When we are fulfilled, we can rest. But the need for expansion will arise again, and our search will proceed. In writing of the soul on its journey, St. Teresa of Avila spoke of the silkworm going through its life stages:

> To see, then, the restlessness of this little butterfly — though it has never been quieter or more at rest in its life! Here is something to praise God for — namely, that it knows not where to settle and make its abode. By comparison with the abode it has had, everything it sees on earth leaves it dissatisfied, especially when God has again and again given it this wine which almost every time has brought it some new blessing. It sets no store by the things it did when it was a worm . . . It has wings now: How can it be content to crawl along slowly when it is able to fly?[15]

May you have whatever strength and courage you need to let your prayer take wings. Remember that the prayer you give as you reach for the authentic one is itself a resource for you on the journey. Sisters and brothers who are making similar journeys can be of great support to you, too. But the greatest challenge and strength will come from knowing that you are always *with* and in many ways *like,* "made in the image of," Mama, the Co-Author of Life, the Creative and Nurturing God, Our Heavenly Father, Friend, the Searcher of Souls, the Healing Presence, Love.

FOR REFLECTION AND ACTION

1. Sit in waiting or disciplined silence for fifteen to twenty minutes once or twice a day for at least a week.

2. Find a Friends' (Quaker) Silent Meeting in your vicinity and attend at least once to experience group waiting silence. (Note: Some Friends' meetings are not modeled on this form of silence, but rather have services quite similar to most other Protestant churches.)

3. Keep a journal of your experience with silence.

4. Do some activity which you engage in regularly, but this time seek to combine the thought of God with your actions. Whenever you notice that you have stopped attending to thoughts of God, bring your focus back, staying attentive to God and the activity simultaneously.

5. Either by yourself or with your family or friends, practice one of the "Mini-Marathon" example sessions (or create one of your own). Give yourself enough time so that you do not need to rush. Record and reflect upon your experience afterward.

6. Turn slowly through the pages of this book, recalling your experience and thoughts as you read the various sections. Now read again the quote from St. Teresa of Avila on page 128. If you identify with the little butterfly, where on the journey do you experience yourself now?

NOTES

1. Violet L. Hodgkin, *Silent Worship* (London: Headley, 1919) 23-24.
2. Ibid., 36, 42, 44.
3. Stanislaw Zielinski, *Psychology and Silence* (Wallingford, PA: Pendle Hill, 1975) 26.
4. Ibid., 28.
5. *Christian Faith and Practice in the Experience of the Society of Friends* (London: Yearly Meeting of the Religious Society of Friends, 1960) #234, #235.
6. Elton D. Trueblood, *The People Called Quakers* (Richmond, IN: Friends United Press, 1971) 125.
7. *Christian Faith . . .* #244.
8. St. Teresa of Avila, *Interior Castle.* E. Allison Peers (trans. and ed.) (New York: Image Books, Doubleday and Co., Inc., 1961) 81.
9. Ibid.
10. Philip Kapleau, *The Three Pillars of Zen* (Boston: Beacon Press, 1965) 238.
11. M. H. Trevor (trans.), *The Ox and His Herdsman: A Chinese Zen Text* (Chiyoda-ku, Tokyo: The Hokuseido Press, 1969) 21.
12. Brother Lawrence, *The Practice of the Presence of God* (New York: Revell, 1976) 23.
13. Ibid., 24.
14. Ibid., 53.
15. St. Teresa of Avila, *Interior Castle* trans. and ed. by E. Allison Peers (Garden City, NY: Image Books, Doubleday and Co., Inc., 1961) 107.

ABOUT THE AUTHOR

Carolyn Bohler is the mother of two children and the Emma Sanborn Tousant Associate Professor of Pastoral Theology and Counseling at United Theological Seminary in Dayton, Ohio. She has served as the minister of a United Methodist church in San Diego, California; Coordinator of Spiritual Life at the School of Theology at Claremont, California; and Chaplain of Simpson College, Indianola, Iowa. She received her Ph.D. and Rel.D. degrees from the School of Theology at Claremont and her B.A. at U.C.L.A. Her first book, *Opening to God: Guided Imagery Meditations on Scripture,* published by The Upper Room in 1977 under the name Stahl, has sold widely. She has recently authored *When You Need to Take a Stand,* published by Westminster/John Knox Press, 1990. Her hobbies include swimming, cooking foods from around the world, and film-going with her husband.

INDEX OF PRAYERS
Topics

INDEX OF PRAYERS
Titles and Styles of Prayers

LuraMedia Publications

Marjory Zoet Bankson, BRAIDED STREAMS: Esther and a Woman's Way of Growing
(ISBN 0-931055-05-09)

SEASONS OF FRIENDSHIP: Naomi and Ruth as a Pattern *(ISBN 0-931055-41-5)*

Carolyn Stahl Bohler, PRAYER ON WINGS: A Search for Authentic Prayer
(ISBN 0-931055-71-7)

Alla Renée Bozarth, WOMANPRIEST: A Personal Odyssey *(ISBN 0-931055-51-2)*

Judy Dahl, RIVER OF PROMISE: Two Women's Story of Love and Adoption
(ISBN 0-931055-64-4)

Judith Duerk, CIRCLE OF STONES: Woman's Journey to Herself *(ISBN 0-931055-66-0)*

Lura Jane Geiger and Patricia Backman, BRAIDED STREAMS: Leader's Guide
(ISBN 0-931055-09-1)

Lura Jane Geiger and Susan Tobias, SEASONS OF FRIENDSHIP: Leader's Guide
(ISBN 0-931055-74-1)

Lura Jane Geiger, Sandy Landstedt, Mary Geckeler and Peggie Oury, ASTONISH ME,
YAHWEH!: A Bible Workbook-Journal *(ISBN 0-931055-01-6)*

Kenneth L. Gibble, THE GROACHER FILE: A Satirical Exposé of Detours to Faith
(ISBN 0-931055-55-5)

Ronna Fay Jevne, Ph.D. and Alexander Levitan, M.D., NO TIME FOR NONSENSE:
Self-Help for the Seriously and Chronically Ill *(ISBN 0-931055-63-6)*

Ted Loder, EAVESDROPPING ON THE ECHOES: Voices from the Old Testament
(ISBN 0-931055-42-3 HB; ISBN 0-931055-58-X PB)

GUERRILLAS OF GRACE: Prayers for the Battle *(ISBN 0-931055-04-0)*

NO ONE BUT US: Personal Reflections on Public Sanctuary *(ISBN 0-931055-08-3)*

TRACKS IN THE STRAW: Tales Spun from the Manger *(ISBN 0-931055-06-7)*

Joseph J. Luciani, Ph.D., HEALING YOUR HABIT: Introducing Directed Imagination, a
Successful Technique for Overcoming Addictive Problems *(ISBN 0-931055-72-5)*

Jacqueline McMakin with Sonya Dyer, WORKING FROM THE HEART: For Those Who
Hunger for Meaning and Satisfaction in Their Work *(ISBN 0-931055-65-2)*

Elizabeth O'Connor, SEARCH FOR SILENCE, Revised Edition *(ISBN 0-931055-07-5)*

Donna Schaper, A BOOK OF COMMON POWER: Narratives Against the Current
(ISBN 0-931055-67-9)

SUPERWOMAN TURNS 40: The Story of One Woman's Intentions to Grow Up
(ISBN 0-931055-57-1)

Renita Weems, JUST A SISTER AWAY: A Womanist Vision of Women's Relationships in
the Bible *(ISBN 0-931055-52-0)*

*LuraMedia is a company that searches for ways to encourage personal growth, shares the excitement
of creative integrity, and believes in the power of faith to change lives.*

7060 Miramar Rd., Suite 104
San Diego, California 92121

LuraMedia ™